Thomas Prestwood Lucas

**Cries from Fiji and sighings from the South Seas**

Thomas Prestwood Lucas

**Cries from Fiji and sighings from the South Seas**

ISBN/EAN: 9783337134150

Printed in Europe, USA, Canada, Australia, Japan

Cover: Foto ©ninafisch / pixelio.de

More available books at **www.hansebooks.com**

# CRIES · FROM FIJI

### AND

# Sighings from the South Seas.

### "CRUSH OUT THE BRITISH SLAVE TRADE."

*Being a Review of the Social, Political, and Religious*
*Relations of the Fijians; a Consideration of the Policy*
*of the English Government; the Prospects of*
*the White Settlers; the Labour Traffic; and*
*the Position and Duties of England to*
*the Islands of the Pacific.*

*Copiously illustrated with Facts and Anecdotes.*

BY

# DR. T. P. LUCAS,

### MELBOURNE.

## DUNN & COLLINS, MELBOURNE.

[*Entered at Stationers' Hall, London.*]

# ERRATA.

Page 26—Line 7, for " neigh-," read neighbour.

.. 26—Line 15, for " do," read does.

,. 62—Line 4. for " natives," read native.

,, 65—Third line from bottom, after " her?" read, Or like the children of tender years, who, enticed by sweetmeats or lollies, leave home to accompany the beggar gipsy woman.

.. 82—Last line, read " At all."

.. 84—Sixth line from bottom. for " She," read The.

# CRIES FROM FIJI

AND

## *SIGHINGS FROM THE SOUTH SEAS.*

————o————

### CRUSH OUT THE BRITISH SLAVE TRADE.

As the traveller journeys among the English-speaking populations of the world, he finds acknowledged on all sides this one fact, that the human family is fallen, and depraved by nature.

Among those nominally Christian, there are heralded two gospels of restoration.

The gospel of Christianity.

The gospel of Civilization.

The gospel of Christianity proclaims two commandments, and promises an eternal Eden.

The first, " Thou shalt love the Lord thy God, with all thy heart, and with all thy mind, and with all thy soul, and with all thy strength."

The second, " Thou shalt love thy neighbour as thyself.'

The gospel of Civilization enunciates two dogmas, and hopes for heaven at last.

The first, " Do your duty in the position in which God has called you, and forget not to return thanks to your Creator."

The second, " Unto others do as you would they should do to you."

The latter gospel is a modified rendering of the former, and is essentially a creed of expediency, but in practice allows its devotees a wide latitude. Every man may do what seemeth right in his own eyes, provided he keep up an appearance of civilized respectability.

Christianity demands a complete surrender of the whole manhood in sacrifice to the Deity ; the heart or affections ; the mind or intelligence ; the soul or life energies, both spiritual and physical ; and the strength or utmost powers of all the capacities.

Civilization advises a respectable allegiance to the Divine, necessitating no self denial, but such as may stamp the man as a respectable citizen.

Christianity demands a perfect morality. Man is to love or regard, and treat his fellow-man, as himself, as far as duty and official responsibilities dictate. The precept is equally strict with man as with woman.

Civilization grants a large degree of licentiousness to man, provided he keep up a certain amount of out-ward respectability. For the sake of decency he must not go too far, or if he err, he must recompense to a degree, so as to suppress the public appeals for redress, those whom he may wrong. But a stricter law is laid down for woman. And too often under this code, man, the wrong-doer, retains his position in society, his foremost seat in the social circle, and his mead of praise in the public life ; while woman, the wronged, is condemned in obloquy and shame to despair and destruction.

The gospel of Christianity prescribes commercial intercourse, but with clean hands, righteous dealings, just weights, fair prices, reasonable profits.

The gospel of Civilization also prescribes commercial intercourse, but allows clever trickery, sharp jobbery, smart dealings, poor articles, adulterated wares, only providing that the dealings must be covered by the cloak of respectability.

The animal nature of man, being essentially selfish, when refined and polished by education, inclines him to the dogmas of Civilization.

The spiritual nature should lead him upwards. But it is so subjected to the animal and selfish, that too often it degenerates downwards.

And so in life, we see three experiences. The animal nature, without education and knowledge, tends to sink man lower and lower—morally, socially, and intellectually.

The gospel of Civilization by education and refinement, seeks to *buoy* man *on the surface* of moral depravity, and to raise him socially and intellectually, to an atmosphere of respectability.

The gospel of Christianity seeks to raise him spiritually

and intellectually to a conception of the highest virtues and to the enjoyment of the purest vitality.

Thus while the spiritual sighs upwards, and the animal gropes downwards, there is necessitated in the breast of every man a mighty struggle. And it is only by super-human aid that the spiritual can rise triumphant, keep the animal in subjection, and advance daily by watchfulness and devotion, in intelligence, experience and refined purity. It is a struggle, a continuous, life-lasting struggle, and one leading the very best men over many falls and stumbles.

Since then purity and righteousness of so high a type are commanded as the acme of human aspirations and intelligence, and since those most highly favoured and most carefully nursed, inculcated and trained in the spirit and teachings of these gifts and graces, have so often failed, or come so vastly short, how shall we judge the heathen, or the wild man just issuing from the stone to the iron age? And the difficulty is increased, when we remember that opinions must vary, even as the higher or lower platforms from whence the judges view the moral and social land-scape. And the different views held upon these matters would cause the several adherents to apply different remedies for the raising the depraved wild man of the South Seas. And so we found was practically the case in Fiji. On the one hand we learned that the Wesleyan missionaries had sought to raise the Viti man by heralding to him the gospel of Christianity; whereas, on the other hand, we learned that the English Government, and the white popula-tion largely, believed in bringing to bear upon the Fijian, only the gospel of Civilization.

It did not require a long period or a very close investigation to discover that the advocates for the refining influences of civilization were inimical to the heralders of the gospel of Christianity. These self-denying men were almost universally blamed for all the ills and woes which had overtaken both black man and white in Viti-land. Although official documents are so often favourable, and although Sir H. Robinson acknowledged that it was through the peaceful conquest of the native races by this agency that Fiji was at length a Crown Colony, yet high officials too often privately sneer and pronounce Missions largely to be a failure. It is the old example of kicking away the ladder by which they climbed. The missionaries were maligned as having large salaries, and as having bought up land for little or nothing. I took special trouble in official quarters to test these questions, and found that the salaries received are lower than those of a carpenter, boatbuilder, or other mechanic of second class ability. I found that of forty-five missionaries, who had spent more or less of their best days in the islands, only three had bought land for their children. And surely, after these philanthropists had given their life energies and denied themselves the comforts of civilized society, not holding their lives dear to them, so as to tame these savages, it would have been a very small return to have received some land on which to settle their children. Yet such was the determined disinterested self-denial of these men, that only three accepted a small portion, and after long service.

It was further given out in official quarters that the Capital was removed from Levuka to Suva because the Wesleyans refused the Government a piece of land, excepting at an outrageous price. Now, in Levuka, a large piece of the land belongs to the Mission. Sir Arthur Gordon was offered the piece of land in question at his own figure, or another piece as a present, the Mission Committee of Management feeling that the acceptance of such would increase the value of their other property. Sir Arthur refused the land, having previously determined to remove to Suva, a place with more accommodation, but as unhealthy a spot as he could very well have selected, and with a rainfall of 110 inches per annum. He wrote and denied that the mission was in any way the cause of the removing the Capital, but to this day officials repeat to the visitor the now stale calumny.

The planters and white settlers generally do not speak evil of the missionaries personally. In fact in early times the mission house was the place of refuge and safety against the warring or cannibal savages, and to-day very many are still houses of hospitality. But they are jealous of the mission. The natives will work for them with a willing service, but only grudgingly and for good wages for the whites. The missionary exerts more power and has more influence than the whites. But even here there is no ground for envy, as the missionaries simply have worked and continue to work disinterestedly for the well-being of the natives. And it is only natural that the natives should acknowledge, with some respect and affection, those to whom they owe so much. While we can hardly wonder that they are distant and mistrusting to the whites, as a whole, seeing how often they have been previously bitten. The whites moreover blame the missions for raising the black man enough to make him troublesome and independent. But, after all, this raising is the result of a civilizing and not a Christianizing influence.

On the whole we found in Fiji, as in other young colonies, much civil and social unrest. The planters had misunderstandings with the sugar companies. The blacks were dissatisfied with the whites, jealous of the importation of Indian coolies, and other ways disaffected. While all classes were more or less dissatisfied with the policy, red-tapeism, and general actions of the Government.

On landing in Fiji, a number of natives came on board the ship and sought to be employed in carrying our luggage. One fine-looking, good-tempered, laughing Fijian obtained my promise to allow him to carry my belongings as soon as I could arrange as to lodgings, &c. By a mistake of the ship's officer, my box was brought up from the hold and sent to the Custom's House. I had to go for it as I wished to stow away in it packages which were loose in my cabin. My engaged native accompanied me. When I got to the Custom's House and explained the situation of affairs, a mere youth half screamed out in tones of authority and dignified pompousness, "Now then, how much tobacco have you in there?" I quietly answered that as I was neither a smoker nor a trader that I had none. "Now then, open the box and turn out the things." My native attendant stood by. "Get away, be off, get out of the road," shouted the Custom's House official. The poor fellow slunk off, but presently came near again. I explained that I had agreed with him to carry my box. "But," answered the official, "he is a lazy fellow and shall not be encouraged." And with that he kicked the black man, and effectually sent him away. After passing my belongings through the Customs, I was directed to a verandahed building where I could get a license to carry a gun. I went up a flight of stairs, and when on the landing asked another official where I could obtain a gun license. "Go down these stairs, and up the next flight of stairs to the door open on the verandah and at the other side of the little gate. This part is private, the other is public." I apologised as a stranger for coming up the wrong stairs, but as I was close to the little gate, which was open, and through which others were passing, I asked to be allowed to go that way, so as to avoid the ascent unnecessarily of another flight of stairs. With a growl he placed himself in my way, and ordered me to go down the stairs, round to the other side, and up the other stairs, and to come to nearly the same point. Such were my first experiences of English officialism on landing in Fiji.

My first interview was with the Government. "Our policy," they stated, "is protection for the native race. We are obliged to protect them from the encroachments of the white people. They look upon the black man as they do upon a plough, as a something solely for their own use and advantage. And they consider it a wrong not to be allowed to force the black man to do their manual labour. Thus we have to protect the natives, or they would die off. Their government is patriarchal, so that the community is dependent on each individual for its existence and prosperity. They are needed to till the ground, and to take them from their villages would be to destroy the family life and thus the maintaining and preservation of the race. We do allow a"portion to be employed, but under certain restrictions and regulations, necessary, as we think, to prevent undue advantage to be taken of them."

"But," I asked, "how about the labour question?" The reply was—"This is nothing more nor less than a slave trade. It is perfectly true that coast tribes kidnap or in other ways obtain men from the inland tribes, and that these are forced to go as recruits, or if they dare to refuse, forfeit their lives for their temerity, the kidnappers receiving the bounty money. And thus, not only are there the evils of the particular kidnapping, but also the origin of feuds and tribal wars. On the whole the whites treat their labourers well, but many die soon after importation. On these grounds we would discourage the labour traffic, and have endeavoured to substitute Indian labour. And, as far as tried, Indian (Coolie) labour has proved a success."

"But," I asked, "why are the whites so dissatisfied with what only appears a philanthropic policy?" "Because," they replied, "in many cases they have lost their all in learning experience. They come down with a little money and no experience, and so loose what little they have, and hence they are dissatisfied with the country, the Government, and with the blacks. Everything is wrong, and everything and everybody is at fault excepting themselves. They expect the natives to do their plantation work, and because they refuse, they cannot speak badly enough."

"Are any Fijians," I asked, "working for the white people, and if so, how many?"

"Yes," was the reply; "out of a male adult population of some 17,000, about six thousand are hired out to work, thus only leaving a necessary quantum to do the needed agricultural and village work."

The general drift of the conversation was the same, painting the Government policy as the most philanthropic philosophy, picturing the Government as persecuted and as martyrs in a good cause, and characterizing the whites as a discontented, selfish, unrighteous community.

As may be imagined, our sympathies were drawn out largely in favour of the Government, and we were strongly prejudiced against the whites. But whatever our thoughts, we determined as yet to form no rash or hasty conclusions. On the contrary, we determined to hear from all sides, opinions, complaints, &c., and thus to endeavour to come at the truth, and to form a common sense unbiassed judgment.

The outcome of our enquiries led to a severe judgment on the policy of the Government. And where their policy is at all of good intention, their actions show vast lacking of brain power and political judgment; for the good out come is largely thwarted by absurd or mischievous qualifying clauses.

Judged by the gospel of Christianity and in the light of philosophy, it is righteous and proper to protect and to seek to improve the native race. Judged by the gospel of civilization, the sooner the weaker go to the wall, the better !

In seeking to protect and preserve the native race, the question arises, what are the wisest and best steps for securing and carrying out such a line of policy? What are the characters and what the characteristic features in the case, and what the protection needed so that these natives should be saved in the race for life with the white man.

As stated by Government, the native governance is a patriarchal one. From the earliest times, and doubtless before their immigration to the Pacific islands, they lived in obedience and servile bondage to chiefs. The rule of these men became despotic and oftentimes tyrannical. A chief appears to have held absolute and tyrannical power, proportionately to his success in war. If fierce, cruel, warlike and aggressively terrible to his foes, he obtained more absolute sovereignty at home. His will was law. His commands were absolute. The lives of his people were in his hands. The daughters of the people were at his mercy and caprice. A man like Thakombau on hearing of a petty theft could order the thief at once to be clubbed ; on hearing of his sister's adultery, he could at once direct that her nose should be slit off ; on needing flesh for feast or for visitors, he could pick from among the people, illegitimate offspring, as victims for cannibalism. And under such a *regime*, every man held his life in his hands, while distrust, hatred, revenge and other allied evils kept the people in a continuous unrest and fear. Such, under many a potentate, was patriarchal government. The people seemed cowed and awed. Traditions and laws held them in crushing bonds. Superstition and a tyrannical patriarchal government crushed them into complete submission. A man ordered to be speared or clubbed would passively submit to his fate ; a woman condemned to be strangled, would unresistingly yield. Cruelty and abomination marked the daily life of the potentate. Cringing submission and fawning flattery that of the subject. Falsehood was looked upon as a necessity. Family life was no longer sacred. The communion was largely a communism, but under a governing and owning master. The personal goods and property and lives of the people were largely at the beck and call of the chieftain. Goods were few and held in common. Any one could beg whatever he or she fancied from a fellow, and to refuse the gift was discourteous, offensive, and in certain cases even criminal. Property was inherited, but landed property was held in little value, excepting as tribal. The chief or even lesser chiefs could demand personal services at call. Life, as stated before, depended on the will or whims of such potentates, and was ever at stake through social differences or through individual, family, or tribal quarrels. Marriage was merely an agreement, and could easily be broken at any moment by mutual consent, and at times the wife would be appropriated by the chief, the husband considering the same as an honor conferred upon him. Thus the common people had no object in life, beyond the merely animal. Eating, drinking and sleeping appeared to be their only end and aim. And of this their food was mostly simple, and was portioned out on the communal system, all sharing according to rank ; their sleep was taken under the protection of warlike weapons, and ever in terrible uncertainty. Such was absolute, tyrannical, patriarchal government. And frightful were the crimes, and fearful to contemplate the condition of these people under such a *regime*.

In certain cases, and to a greater degree in former times, the people, through enterprising leaders or because their chiefs were less successful or less enterprising in warlike aggressions, obtained a controlling hand. Under these circumstances, the chief had to listen to one or more counsellors. And if his rule became too biting, his subjects could leave him, and migrate to another ruler, or a blood relation, instigated by the tribe or clan, would club the man and so end his tyranny. The assassin would then reign in his victim's stead. But even under such modified government, the rule was always despotic, and though prevented from going to such great lengths, yet the lives and persons of individuals were never safe, and all the evils connected with this form of slavery were in arrogant reign. Slavery ! yes, slavery. The patriarchal system of government is always a more or less mitigated form of slavery. The communism destroys individual rights of property. The patriarch or chief is the real and only man of independence and means. The properties of his subjects are a mere nothing, and are at their master's caprice. Their persons are at his service, either for aggression or for social or other service. His fiat is law. Individual liberty is restricted and freedom is lost. All the interests are communal, and the whole communism is at the mercy of the whims and temper of the lord and father. Individual effort, individual ambition, individual energy is lost in the one body of which this man is the head. The patriarch or chief has to care for his subjects or tribe ; but this care is more often only a selfish one. A taking care to procure absolute necessities demanded to his retaining the number and wealth of followers. And it is simply a directing the individual efforts, to the one conserving for the whole, and that whole for the aggrandisement and power of the head. To make matters worse and the slavery a greater bondage, the patriarch or chief has to rely for aid on a number of personages, who are advanced to certain positions or rank, or who hold the same as hereditary. These, while oppressing the people generally for their chief's demands and dues, never neglect to oppress and to cajole for their own selfish objects and aims. And thus it is that whereas the tyranny of one despot might be bearable, balanced as it must largely be, in his own safety and interests, that of underlings becomes infinitely more severe and crushing, the oppression bearing relative proportion to the aims and ambitions of such in power. In fact, it is impossible to imagine a patriarchal government, heathen or even civilized, excepting as a communal bondage and personal slavery. Perhaps the most righteous patriarchal governance was that of Abraham. Yet under it. the land was his, the cattle and camels and sheep were absolutely his own ; the servants were his ; the whole community had to follow him to war. In this example of patriarchal governance, we see the outcome of the system under a righteous man. And in it we see the destruction of individual liberties and ambitions, to the securing the one end, the aggrandisement and power of Abraham and his heirs for ever. And whereas this dispensation might have had its advantages in the early ages of the world, and while men's minds and experiences were young, yet as the descendents of Abraham increased in numbers and in knowledge and experience, they threw off the patriarchal communism, fostered the family life, recognised the individual manhood, and assigned to each their righteous standing and importance. And thus they became a nation, an impossibility under patriarchal rule, which is distinctively tribal and autocratic. The patriarchal rule is such that it is necessarily too limited in its area and influence to become national. And as the history of the past has ever proved, peoples have only become nations as they have discarded the tribal and patriarchal, and by conquest and alliances increased in number and influence under a monarchy or republican government.

In a word, a nation becomes great and influential in proportion to the sum total of the wealth, power and influences of its individual members. A tribe under patriarchal rule only becomes great and influential in proportion to the influence and power of its chief. And what show has the one against the many? In the national system every inducement is given and every protection afforded to individual and family talent and righteous ambition, while in the chieftain or tribal, all individual effort and aspiration is lost in the communal and destroyed in the despotic.

The avowed policy of the English Fijian Government, as related to me by one of its highest officials is—The preservation and protection of the native race by securing to them their old patriarchal government. By hedging in and defending the same against the crafts and selfishness of the whites, and by upholding the power of the chiefs.

Such a policy may at first sight appear philanthropic, but it is practically fratricidal! Under existing relations, it reminds one of the conduct of Joab and Amasa. Appearing before him in the light of a friend, and greeting him with a kiss, as he grasped him by the beard, "Art thou in health, my brother?" he plunged the dagger into his heart. And while the Government are saying to the Fijian, "Hail, brother!" and frowning upon the whites because of their grumbling, they, at the same time, are plunging the dagger of destruction with sure and steady aim into the heart of the Fijian.

To enable an outsider to see the correctness of the argument, it is necessary to review briefly the character and capabilities of the Fijian; and secondly, the means adopted by the Government for their carrying out their preservative and protective policy.

It must be remembered that the Fijians have just emerged from a state of the deepest moral degradation and despotic bondage. And this *entirely the work of missionary effort*. None can deny this. A man knowingly to deny a fact must be a fool. Wisdom, philosophy and manly straightforwardness are not in him. He may not like the fact, or he may not like the actors in the background, but it is absurdity to deny the fact itself. And in Fiji, it is patent and palpable to any person who chooses to look philosophically and unbiassed into the matter. Sir Hercules Robinson, in 1875, said, " The great social advances which have already been made within the last forty years from savage heathenism, are due to the self-denying and unostentatious labours of the Wesleyan Church."* History affirms, and records which cannot be contradicted, show, that during this present century the Fijians were sunken more deeply into the slough of degradation than they had ever been before. And this largely through English influence.

About the year 1804, twenty-seven convicts escaped from New South Wales and landed in Fiji. These men introduced fire-arms, sunk to the degradation of the natives, and by their superior knowledge of the arts of civilized nations, exerted almost a kingly sway over the parts where they settled. At Mbau and Rewa they allied with the chiefs, and in return for influence and hospitality, assisted them, by means of their superior weapons and knowledge, to increase their rule ; and as a consequence the despotism

* " At Home in Fiji."—Miss Gordon Cummins.

and arrogance of their now more independent and strength-
ened sway. The outcome was an almost absolute despotic
patriarchal sway, overshadowing a reign of terror, and as a
consequence a most degraded and vile bondage ridden communism. Life was uncertain, sacrificed singly or in
multitudes as occasion dictated. Cruelty in its worst forms
was practised. Law, excepting as the caprice of the chiefs,
was almost unknown. A man's hand might be against
every man, and any man's hand might be against him, as
authority or passion willed. Woman was degraded to a
menial and sold or driven away as policy or fancy dictated.
It was unsafe to leave the borders or precints of one tribe,
or even township, to pass into the domains of another. If
open warfare was acknowledged, life was sought openly : if
peace was the reign, it needed chieftain influence and guidal
protection, and too often even then treachery and villany
secured flesh for the oven and a meal for the covetous.
The whole land was but a sum total of habitations of
cruelty. The village had its stone, where the brains of the
victims were dashed out in offering to the gods. One man
would get hold of either arm of the victim, and rushing him
along, dash his head against the stone, scattering brains
and blood. The township had its tree where innumerable
notches recorded the sacrifice of the slain. The public oven
in the midst of their habitations for ever raised its polluted
smell to the skies. The chief increased the number of his
wives, thrashing them periodically with his own hand, to
keep them in terror and submission. Strangulation was an
accomplished art. A noose would be thrown over the neck

of the victim, who often passively yielded without a struggle. A man on either side would grasp the end of the rope (a roll of native cloth), and placing a foot each, in the armpits, would simultaneously pull. The tongue forced from the mouth, would instantly hang out, and in a moment the deed was done.

And the English criminal escapees, educated in English civilization, but punished for more or less heinous or trivial infringements of the laws regulating the same, made matters ten thousand times worse, by the powers they gave the chief and the fearful examples they set before the natives. Numbers of wives and numbers of children seemed to be their chief aim, and to-day villages of half-castes cry from Fiji, against the wrongs inflicted on helpless heathen by civilized (?) Englishmen.

A gentleman assured me that when in 1852 he landed at Levuka, he dared not walk a mile along the shore, nor dared he to go at all towards the interior.

But missionaries went with their lives in their hands, and excepting in one or two instances, and that largely through their own temporary forgetfulness or neglect of ordinary caution, were preserved alive. They went heralding the gospel of Christianity, they lived self-denying Christian lives. The power of Heaven came down upon the natives—the mercies of the Most High overtook the people, and the lion became the lamb—the murderer and adulterer, the humble truster and believer in Jesus. And what was the final outcome. Tribe after tribe accepted the lotu (Christianity), threw away their deadly weapons, ceased their broils, learned to live in peace, filled the churches and the schools, buried their taste for man eating, and sought with all their powers to learn and to practice the religion of Jesus. And all this before civilization could come in to the aid. What was it that modified the terrors practised by Thakombau in his later years, and which effectually at last broke down his tyranny and vileness? Answer, the gospel of Christianity. And this he acknowledged as he lay dying. "Faith! Wonderful faith! Saved by faith!" He then exerted himself and prayed aloud with wonderful fervour and power; and laying back, quietly passed away. A white man who stated that the Fijians had not brains enough to comprehend and to live Christianity, said, "But I must acknowledge *Thakombau was a Christian*." Missionaries reduced the language to a written form, and taught the people reading and writing. Missionaries taught the people how to sing. Their war songs and national ditties are the veriest doggerel, and are poured forth with a strain in a a tone something between grunting and a snoring. But the missionaries composed hymns (the Wesleyan hymn book contains 168), and taught the natives the old country tunes, and now they can sing with a power and pathos, which would send a thrill through any English congregation, and which would put many a choir to shame. I had a most pleasing and affecting instance of the same. I was travelling by boat from Rewa township to Mbau. The journey was along a tidal river, and partly by sea, eight hours. The wind was favorable, and as we sped along to my astonishment and pleasure, the boat's crew struck up a hymn in Fijian:—

> All hail the power of Jesu's name,
> Let angels prostrate fall ;
> Bring forth the royal diadem,
> And crown Him Lord of all.

I could not speak Fijian, and they could not speak English, and there was no interpreter. Yet I knew the tune and recognized the metre, and felt the influence and spirit of the song. Our spirits were as one, as animated by the inspiration on those Fijian waters, I joined in the song, and impelled them on in energy and earnestness. And although our words were different, our language was the same, as the angels on their wings wafted our song to Heaven.

My feelings as I went back in thought, may be better imagined than expressed. Savages, and the offspring of cannibals, and the near relatives of sacrificed cannibal victims, going in peace and assurance to their old and hereditary enemy, Mbau, and singing songs and praises to the King of Peace. Men whom I would not be ashamed to count as friends and brethren. And all this transformation, the result of missionary enterprize.

The Fijian reminded me of the public school boy of England of old. Youths, from fifteen to seventeen years of age, would exercise a species of terrorism over the small boys. Friendships among the lads were easily made, easily broken. Deep feeling among the young was transitory and flashing, and made little appreciable difference in their lives and habits. Sorrow was momentary, love was childish, shallow and fickle. The cares of life did not burden or trouble the youthful mind. Sufficient for the day was the evil thereof. The real philosophy of things was as yet a distant viewed theme. A kind of communism was virtually acknowledged, so that when any boy obtained a parcel of cakes and good things, he was regularly besieged by beggars, and accounted a mean fellow and a glutton if he did not divide the spoil. In a word, the mental capacities and ideas were only developed to a limited extent. The boy of sixteen thinks differently and views things in a very different light to what a man of forty does. Yet the boy of sixteen could comprehend the spiritual and understand the great truths of Christianity and the moral law. His brain powers are not developed to the extent they would be at the age of forty. And hence he could not think and judge at sixteen as he would at forty,

As far as I could judge, the mental capacities of the Fijians are on an average, and their ideas had developed equally, with those of ordinary English school-boys foom fifteen to seventeen. They are specially restricted in mathematical mind. But they can count up to a hundred thousand, having to count thousands of yams at the great feasts, and as tribute. They have to calculate slowly the simplest monetary transactions. They can appreciate a rise in value, but cannot comprehend the reason for a fall in the money market. For some time everything was offered in barter for sixpence, until European competition led on to a shilling. And now a native will ask one shilling for a dozen or so of lemons or oranges, while another will ask no more for a large basket full. A man with a sovereign and wanting commodities, will go to a shop or store, and first of all change his gold for twenty shillings. If the article he requires cost sixpence or three-pence, he will again change a shilling for these smaller coins. He thus gains confidence, and will slowly and cautiously pay in each separate coin, as he receives the article of equivalent value. If a native be sent for change for a five pound note, he will almost assuredly return and declare that the change is not correct. He gets puzzled in counting it, or possibly he may drop a coin, just as a thoughtless English boy might do. If the Englishman, who gave the change, is firm and confident that he gave the exact amount, and especially if he can bring corrobora-tive proof, then the bearer of the change must explain and resolve the difficulty, or be accounted by his fellows as a thief and a rogue. These errors so often occur, that many of the whites, judging severely, count all the Fijians as thieves and lazy rascals, whereas the error is oftener than not, through the lack of intelligence.

Like English schoolboys, the Fijians are full of merri-ment, and are likewise extremely loquacious. Give them biscuits, and a whole company will laugh and talk in the loudest and utmost confusion. I had but to enter a native village, show my butterfly net and its object, and my collecting box with the specimens pinned out, and amidst greetings of the loudest laughter, and most extreme signs of pleasure and approbation, all would essay to assist me in my natural history search. And the young women especially, on capturing a grasshopper or a spider, would triumphantly bring the capture, the whole company simply screaming with delight.

Like the schoolboys again, they are terrible beggars. Share and share alike is not always satisfaction. A man with a poor shirt will fancy a better one, which his neighis wearing, and proposes an exchange, which it is neither custom or etiquette to refuse. A man may earn a pound, when this one fancies something, and that one needs something, until the poor fellow's pound disappears in shillings, scarcely leaving one or more for his own use. And as a further analogy to the public school boy ideas, the chief as the dux, monitor or prefect, over the small boys or fags, may and do come on the man for the tit-bits or lion's share. A chief's rights by custom and law are ten per cent. And thus it is, that the patriarchal communism destroys all individual ambition among the Fijians. And without individual ambition and emulation, there is no stimulus to personal effort, either physical or mental, beyond what is enforced by the communal, or beyond what may be suggested by the requirements of the hour. Hence a Fijian with plenty of food, with little necessity for clothing, passes his life in an indolent dream. For, owing to his governmental laws and customs, he is neither fired with the ambition of amassing property, nor with the desire to rise in the social, mental or political scale, beyond the place where birth and circumstances have placed him. If he wants a new handkerchief for a sulu, or if he desires to buy bread, or a knife, or a lamp, or a similar trinket, he will dive for coral, or search the reef for shells, and these he will offer for sale to ships' crews or to white visitors. Others will sell bananas or cocoa-nuts, while others again will work at manual labour. But their needs satisfied, they are uncertain as to their continuance as servants. Further, Fijians are proud, and partly through pride, and fear of being satired by their kinsfolk, even as school boys would act, they are exceedingly diffident at working within their own township or tribe. As children, they have little moral [courage, and cannot bear ridicule or satire. But many, away from their native village, are willing and ready to work, and prove able and efficient servants.

Much has been said of the advancing and increasing capacities of mankind. It is urged that the stone age men are of vastly smaller capacities than are those of [these civilized times. And some naturalists go so far as to tabulate a Homo pygmœus, as precedent to the Homo sapiens. In the South Seas we get the man of the stone age; we see others passing into the iron age. How, then, do their capacities appear in relation with those of polished, refined Europeans? On the whole I believe the capacities of mankind to be equal, that is in striking an all-round average. And doubtless, this has been the case from the beginning. I measured the heads of a boat's crew of Fijians (eight men), round the temples. They measured $22\frac{1}{2}$ to $25\frac{1}{2}$ inches. Now this is a good English average. The circumference thus measured, bore relation to the size and weight of the whole body. It was not a key to the mental capacities, but it was the key to the nerve or brain-centre capacities. The man with the smallest head was quite a genius for music, and was the precentor in the church of his native township, but he had the smallest body. The brain-centre capacities are developed according as they are exercised or called into play in active life. They cannot all be developed largely. The calling any particular centre or centres into large development means a diminishing or cramping the development of others. In the South Sea Islanders of the stone age, the physical factors are from generation to generation being called into play. Hence they are largely developed, fine muscles, strong limbs, &c. Particular features are most highly intuitioned. Riggling through the bush with snake-like fleetness and quiet; climbing trees with the agility of a monkey; using the bow and arrow, or aiming with the ponderous club; resisting the influences of the weather in an almost nude condition : the powers of swimming and diving ; the arts of rude navigation. But all these powers call up a certain and that a large amount of the brain capacity. Then in the mental arena, the native is intuitioned as a child of nature. He notices the products of nature, studies their uses, uses their similes in argument. Thus his capacities are drawn upon both physically and mentally up to the extent of those capacities. But when he passes on from the stone to the iron age, he draws less on particular capacities, the rude arts often so highly perfected, cease to be a necessity, and so become lost. But in place of these non-utilized capacities, he can begin to learn reading,

writing, and the simple rules of arithmetic. And as
generations pass, as shown by the negroes, the people
might become more highly and intellectually developed, by
a continued training in that direction, but at the loss of
physical prowess or rude astute perfections of former days.
In a word, the capacities of the people are the same in the
latter generation as in the former, but the relative development of the various capacities are shifted. And doubtless
this has ever been the case with mankind. The physical
capacities of the wild man are developed far beyond those
of the scholar or the civilized man; but the mental
capacities of the scholar or civilized man are far more
highly developed than those of the untutored savage.
Nevertheless on the average, the sum total of their respective developments indicate a like amount, on the
average, of all-round nerve or brain development, size for
size, according to the relative proportions of the body.
There is no increase of brain matter necesssary to the
development of intellectual capacities. It is simply
developed to the full in that particular direction in preference
to others not tuitioned into play.

The whites complain that the Fiji man is lazy and many
call him or look upon him as a dog, fit only for eating and
sleeping and causing trouble. But after all, they act as
the whites themselves would under the circumstances, only
ten times better. If the whites had all their wants
supplied, if personal possessions were an impossibility, and
if work brought little reward, they certainly would not
work. The marvel is not, why so many Fijians decline

work, but how it is that so many do work. They have little need to work, they have little reward for work, they are often snubbed and treated as dogs, perhaps not molested, but sneered at and snubbed, and satire is worse than cuffs to the Viti man, by those for whom they do work. What wonder then, that so many prefer the easy trading and the independence, to the heavy manual labour, and the too often servile bondage! Yet because of this state of things, rendered worse as we shall shew shortly, by the Government, the blacks are spoken of badly, and held in contempt by the whites.

The patriarchal communal system in two ways specially makes against the natives seeking to work or to amass substance or wealth. When any work among themselves is required to be done, all the men of a village or tribe will be ordered out by the chief to assist in that work. When in Rewa, I saw an instance of this. The chiefs were about to return from a council which had been held. All hands were set on to clear the village paths of weeds and grass. It was ludicrous and most amusing to watch a company of some 300 men, in schoolboy fashion, some with spades, some with hoes, and others with any implement, even to a stick or knife, whichever they could command, seeking to clear the few weeds from a narrow road, of some ten or twelve feet wide, for a distance of less than a quarter of a mile. They set about it without any apparent order or definite plan. Each one struck at a weed wherever he might fancy, and this large band of able-bodied men, so pompous in ceremony, would accomplish less real work than two or three sturdy Englishmen could have done in the same time. And that in a much more slovenly manner. But this to the Fijian mind is the correct method of working, and hence for a European to ask him to perform manual labour, and not himself and all hands join in, is almost, if not quite, an insult to the native ideas. And further, the communal system, which teaches them to beg from and to give to one another, leads them on to try the same with the English. The natives are however beginning to learn that the English will not thus part with their property. And that they for value require equivalent value. But yet the idea is rooted in their minds by tradition and custom, that goods should be in common. And if work should be communal and goods communal, why should they alone be asked to work, and for the benefit alone and the amassing wealth alone to the white man. Trade is now stepping in, but yet the natives, where they think they can succeed, will beg. And it is only by satire or by returning the compliment that they can be made to desist. I stayed one night and was hospitably entertained at a native village, one of the latest to lotu, and until comparatively recently unsafe to visit. I was in the most cool manner asked for my watch. I nodded my head, laughed, and answered, "To-morrow." The joke pleased and I was troubled no further. An Englishman living near related to me a most amusing experience. He visited a chief, who professed very great friendship and regard. But this man and his people proved most irrational beggars. The more he gave, the more they begged. This, viewed from the standpoint of the English

school boy, was only natural. As children, they were glad
to get hold of the white man's, to them, curios. He found
himself in a fix, not deeming it policy, under the circumstances, to refuse the polite demands. His only remedy
was to imitate the traveller in his relations with the Indian
chief. That chief who protected and acted as a great friend
to the traveller would periodically relate, how that in his
dreams, the great spirit had awarded him various valuables,
possessions of the white man : and the traveller had in
policy to present him with them. At length, when the
dreaming became frequent and unbearable, he met the
Indian with a like complaint. He had dreamed, and the
great spirit had directed that the best piece of land and of
large dimensions should be given to the traveller. On
relating this to the chief, his face witnessed the angered
and restrained feelings within his breast, when he answered,
" Take them, my friend, but let us have no more dreaming." And so the white man belaboured in Fiji, turned
round, gave no breathing time, but rapidly asked for everything he saw in the possession of one after another. He
was never again subjected to begging in that township.
The joke was too practical.

Fijians again, as English school boys, do not appear to
know depths of sorrow or love. The finer heaven-like
passions are not strongly developed. They may and do
have paroxysms of sorrow, but they are neither lasting nor
deep. A woman in a native village which I visited had
shortly before lost her child   A gentleman, who hap-
pened to be present at the time, told me that she set

up a hideous wail, and kept it up for two hours. Soon
after there was little or no sign of grief. And so it is with
English children. Their grief is paroxysmal and to them
for the moment crushing, but it is soon over. And in both
cases it is demonstrative. Whereas the deep crushing
sorrow, or the unassuaged lasting grief so frequently seen
in the more intellectually matured English, is wanting or
almost unknown among the South Sea Islanders.

And so with love. Here they do not seem to be demonstrative, excepting in polite words. I saw a large number
of the inhabitants of a village return from a journey of
some days by sea. Their boat was laden with food and
other articles. They busied themselves, rather in carrying
their effects into the village, than in saluting their relatives
and friends whom they had not seen for days. A husband
would stop a minute to shake hands (an introduced custom),
with his wife, and each to pass a smile. A little lad of
seven or eight years ran to his mother. Both for a
moment showed their pleasure, the boy in dancing around
and looking up at his mother, the mother in putting her
arms round the lad and pressing him fondly to her breast.
But even this was temporary. I saw no kiss bestowed.
A sniff up the nose takes the place of the kiss in Fiji. A
person presses his nose against another's hand and sniffs ;
this shows respect. He acts the same against the cheek,
and this betokens affection. But, for the most part,
although I inquisitively watched the returning ones
come to their homes, the salutations were common-place,
or a formal shake of the hand. Plenty of talking,

plenty of laughing, but little besides. And so with slight exception, we find this state of things, little demonstration of affection, among English school boys. It is stated that these people have no word in their language for gratitude. An English boy knows the word, but very seldom, or only to a limited degree, understands or experiences the *depths* of gratitude. A Polynesian expressed great fondness for a white baby, and so was engaged entirely as nurse. And it is well-known that English children, from babies upward, get on far better with the natives than with white servants. Their sympathies are nearer akin. And a native will quiet and amuse a child where a European fails. This man was hired for a certain period, and vowed that when his time was up, he would engage again, as he could not leave his loved baby. But, alas! when the time arrived, his boasting was gone; and, as if ashamed of satire on his conduct, he departed unheralded and by stealth. I was highly amused with a village of native boys. Curious and prying, they came to me, got me ferns, took my net and caught insects, and carried some papers I had. Each one wanted to help. And for every favor I bestowed, or notice I took, the recipient would say " Thank you! " Thank you-s were numerous, and doubtless as full of meaning as many a one uttered by the more favoured English boy. Yet many white people argue that, as the Fijians are so deficient in these passions, that they cannot rise to the spiritual, and that hence the efforts of missionaries are futile, except to generate hypocrisy and to foster pride. This, at first sight, might appear feasible. But a review of the school-boy life, analogous, as we stated, with the Fijian, will demonstrate otherwise. School boys and Fijians are both highly spiritual. They are both easily impressed, and are not troubled with doubts and inimical philosophical creeds. Both can love up to their capacities, and both can understand the principle of vicarious propitiatory sacrifice as the expression of, and as actuated by, love. Love, the sheet-anchor of the Christian religion. And while the school boy has not the capacities, either of intellect or of this noblest passion, maturely developed, yet he can, and often does, attain to a consistent profession and possession of true godliness. And so the Fijian. He has not the capacities of the educated, intelligent, and experienced Englishman ; but he has a capacity to understand a plan so simple that the wayfaring man, though a fool, need not err therein.

But a possession of religion necessitates a keen struggle and continuous effort to retain and increase. And it is well-known to every observer that profession often belies possession, and that, through weariness and unwatchful-ness, even Europeans become lukewarm and careless, while many altogether fall away. And in judging the Fijians, allowance should be made for their less developed capaci-ties, for their numerous temptations, for the hereditary evil tendencies of their nature, and for their natural puerile weaknesses. The example of the white people, whom they know are higher in the social scale, is often most deleteri-ous. The missionaries teach them, as children should be taught, with Puritan severity and rule. The Sabbath is for them in letter, as well as in spirit, a day of rest. But the Europeans largely set a contra example, and so agitate the minds of these little ones.

Taught by the missionaries, they endeavour to an extent unprecedented in civilised, nominally Christian countries, to live as far as knowledge and capacities lead, Christian lives. Every morning numbers assemble for family prayer. On the Sabbath, the churches are filled with devout worshippers. Anxious to see for myself, I attended the native services. Immediately on the minister and white visitors entering the church, the congregation, devoutly kneeling, chanted a prayer, asking for the blessing of the Almighty on the service, that they might be profited and blessed. After the opening prayer, they chanted the Lord's Prayer and the Apostles' Creed. Before the delivery of the sermon, they chanted the Fourth Commandment, Remember the Sabbath Day, &c. The chanting was commenced by the women, and then taken up and carried on by the men. The whole ceremony was most impressive and solemn. I listened to a native local preacher or teacher, as he urged upon his hearers, the value of their privileges. " Not long ago," he said, " we were like people shut up in a dark house—all the doors barred, and no windows. We had no outlook. All was dark. Prison darkness, which could be felt, surrounded us all. And we were helpless, lost, and miserable. But the light shone forth. The doors of the dungeon were opened. The light shone in upon us. And now we see the full sunshine of gospel-day. But many of us are forgetful. We do not embrace this light. We prefer the darkness. Or we like the twilight. Wherefore should we neglect such glorious privileges? And what punishment shall we deserve if we allow this glorious light and liberty to pass from us unheeded?" I was simply astounded by what I saw and heard.

While at Mbau, I witnessed a number of mekes or native dances. The men dance alone. The women likewise dance with each other. The movements of the body and of the limbs are in perfect symmetry. They are extremely graceful and most artistic.

The strangers had to be feasted by the townspeople. I counted seventeen pigs, roasted whole, carried past me to the meal. And yet, although there was so much excitement, although it was a public holiday, the week-night preaching service was attended by hundreds.

When at Ovalau, I received an invitation to attend a native missionary meeting. Before the day in question, the people of the village sent to their minister, and asked permission for the meeting to be put off for a day or two. They stated that they had not money sufficient for what, in their hearts, they wished to give. Three steamers, one a pleasure party steamer, were expected, and they wished to secure these opportunities, so as to sell coral and curios. And then they would have money for the missionary meeting. As desired, the meeting was deferred. On the morning of the day chosen, I had the pleasure, with three other visitors, of visiting that village. The chief had made a feast for strangers. The visiting natives were treated according to their rank or precedence. A spokesman

regretted that the feast was not more varied or choice. But
the visitors were most welcome, and he hoped they would
partake of the good things in the same spirit as that in
which they were given. A suitable reply and compli-
mentary speech was made. The feast began. Fish soup,
boiled fish, ndalo, yams, sweet puddings. Portions were
awarded to the whites. Afterwards the natives feasted
with a will. After the feast came the missionary meeting.
A native gave a brief address. He stated the good they
themselves had received from the lotu. He drew attention
to the South Sea Islanders still in heathenism : and he
wound up by urging them all to give liberally.

I expected to see a number of speakers get up with the
object, as is necessary in English audiences, of inciting to
good works and to liberal gifts ; but I was mistaken. In
a business manner they looked at matters. The collection
was at once called. The chief got up, and in a stately
grace, as a child proud of success, put on the plate eleven
shillings. Then others stepped up with offerings. Then
the little girls, nicely decorated with flowers and ferns,
walked up and put their sixpenny and threepenny pieces
on the plate. There was joy among the poor people of
that native village, as, like the Jews of old, they brought
up and poured forth their gifts into the treasury ; almost
their all. The collection amounted to three pounds nine-
teen shillings and sixpence.

The village was so poor, that the cocoa-nut trees had to
be tabooed (forbidden) to pay the Government taxes. The
English were anxious to taste the young nuts. But no ;

they were forbidden. No one dared to climb. At last, a bonny-looking young woman said, "I can manage it for you." And so she ran to the chief. In a few minutes she returned, and stated that, in honour of the white guests, the taboo was taken from one tree. Permission given, a native looked up, and judging of the nuts as they grew, selected the tree with the finest fruit. He crawled and climbed with the most perfect ease—a far better gymnast than any English actor. In a few minutes, nuts were thrown down, unhusked, opened, and the guests refreshed by the beautiful cool milk. Such was the hospitality, and such the liberality we witnessed in a poor village. Poor in this world's goods ; but rich in gifts and graces too often lacking in more refined and more highly favoured communities. And like instances might be multiplied.

One thousand and seventy teachers, and two thousand and ninety-seven school teachers, are distributed among the various towns and villages. These men are supported by the natives, and get a salary of twelve to twenty shillings a quarter. And often the towns are too poor to pay even that moiety. And yet, such is their love of the work, that they remain at their posts, even though poor, rather than be led away by promise of higher wages.

In 1875 it was proposed to open a mission in New Britain. The matter was laid before a number of Fijian teachers. Nine volunteered to go. Seven of these were married. The British Consul interfered, considering it his duty to explain to them the dangers they were running. He sought to dissuade them from their enterprise ; but they were not to be moved from their purpose. They stated that they knew the difficulties and dangers, and if they got killed, well ; if they lived, well : Go they must. One of the wives was then urged not to go—not to risk her life. She answered : " I am like the outrigger of a canoe—where the canoe goes, there you will surely find the outrigger." And they went. Four were mur lered by the cannibals for the ovens. And yet the gaps were soon filled up, and fresh teachers continued to volunteer. When we remember that the Fijians are naturally cowards, we are astounded at the valour and heroism. No forces of civilization could work such wonders. Their lives in their hands, and the club and the ovens awaiting them ! Yet they go. Love to enemies. Christian philosophy. Heavenly purity. And to-day some 3000 more or less tamed cannibals witness to the self-denying love of the white missionary, and of these men in the New Britain Mission.

Although naturally of strong passions, considering their surroundings, their weaknesses, and their temptations, these people keep remarkably moral and temperate. They not only abstain from intoxicating drinks, but many of them have joined a " Blue Ribbon " movement to abstain from the Yangona and tobacco. This Yangona is a native drink, of which they are very fon l, and which simply renders the legs helpless, without affecting the head, other than with a pleasurable satisfied sensation. In travelling by boat from Suva to the Rewa River, the wind was against us, and the

two natives, Kandavu boys, had to pull the whole distance
of twelve miles. A gentleman in the company had taken
bottles of beer for the whites, and had considerately
provided bottles of tea and milk for the natives. Seeing
beer, they were suspicious, and the one persistently refused
to drink the tea, while the other was with great difficulty
persuaded to swallow a portion. They were assured that
the tea had been specially provided for them, but the
bottles of beer made them fear treachery or a practical
joke. And I was agreeably surprised and astounded to
see how the one refused any drink at all, lest he should
err, even, working hard as he was, under the discomfiture
of a tropical sun.

For a people, and this chiefly owing to the missionaries'
teaching, they are most circumspect as regards the
Europeans. The young women by their own regulations,
are only allowed to go out two and two. Those whites who
set the disgraceful example of living in concubinage, have
to appropriate imported Tongan, Samoan, or Rotumah
women. While a Fijian prostitute is most rare. I only
heard of one confirmed case of an English girl being seduced
by a Fijian. And this was one of terrible retribution, and
occurred some little time ago. A young Englishman
visited Kandavu, and there lived prodigal and rakish.
Some time after, he was commissioned to get labour boys.
He went again to Kandavu, and, as an inducement, promised
wives, and among them the hand of his own sister. To the
astonishment of every one, in a very short time he returned
with a number of the boys. Some months afterwards, the

young man's family found that the daughter had been seduced, and furthermore by a Fijian. The man openly acknowledged his guilt, gloried over his revenge, stating that it was the avowed agreement of the boys, to accept the labour bonuses, so as to gain an opportunity to be revenged on the young man, for seducing women of their township. And he dared the friends to bring the matter forward before the Crown authorities. They thought and adopted the wiser and more discreet plan of silence, and sent the girl away to Sydney.

During the old *regime*, woman was powerless before a Chief, but now that Christianity has enlightened the people the matter is changed. Only a few days previous to my visit, a woman of Christian profession fought bravely with her fists, and beat off a very high chief and Government official, who sought to tamper with her. In fact, the Chiefs are the greatest sinners, being placed in power by the Government, and armed with privileges (a permit to drink alcoholic drinks, to have many wives, &c.), which act deleteriously to the small capacity intelligence. A little power is dangerous, and puffs up weak intellect, and so the ill-awarded powers damage the holders morally, socially, and physically. But worst of all, the poor people have to suffer·

Thus when all things are taken into consideration, it must be acknowledged that Christianity has done a great deal for Fiji. And often in spite of bad examples, where better should have been expected. Out of about 120,000 natives, the Wesleyan body have an attendance of some 100,000, and a membership of 35,000. And although there are black sheep among them as in every flock, yet many of them are earnestly striving to live better lives and to be true Christians.

Fijians, as schoolboys, have not highly developed mechanical minds. Their wants are few and simple, and so the brain in this particular direction has not been led to development.

Again like schoolboys they are highly inquisitive, and to a fault. Perhaps this is now their worst national failing. They seem uneasy and unhappy until they can satisfy their curiosity. A storekeeper commissioned one of them to take eight business letters to Suva, a distance of a few miles. The man asked to be told the contents of each. He was curtly denied, but assured they were not about himself. He refused to take the letters. The two natives who accompanied me in my tour inland, asked a planter why I collected ferns, insects and birds. To make tea in Sydney, was the planter's jocular reply. Scarcely knowing whether it was so, or whether it was a joke, they asked no further, but simply sought to read from his countenance, what they were uncertain of in words. But though extremely inquisitive, their inquisitiveness in only childish, and a mere superficial explanation and comprehension will satisfy their curiosity.

The Fijians are of a keen nervous temperament. They seem to live very near the spirit land. Their gods in the days of heathenism were spirits. It has been suggested in scientific circles, that as the human brain becomes more developed, second sight or impressions from the spirit world would be

more easily aud often perceived.  But here facts disprove
theory.  Among the Fijians we get a far more keen per-
ception, through nervous influences, than we do in more
refined advanced intellects.  Even the Australian abori-
gines could foretell the advent of a ship days before
sighted.  A young Fijian student, anxious to become a
successful teacher, studied hard.  He got some disease
which those around him could not understand.  His head
was very hot, and he experienced great pain.  Lassitude,
and so to speak, a giving up the ghost, a resigning all
energy and struggle after life, came on, and he apparently
died.  He was gone so far as only to give a breath every
two or three minutes.  When all believed him to be gone,
and were preparing to perform the last ceremonies, he
suddenly rose up and said:  " I thought I was gone ; but
I have come back again to urge you all to be watchful and
earnest in prayer."  He then dropped back and died.
Another teacher, apparently in good health on the Thurs-
day or Friday, said :   " I must get all things in order—I
shall preach my farewell sermons on Sunday ; give tickets
and arrange church matters on Monday ; for on Tuesday
I shall stretch all sail and fly away."  He carried out these
intentions.  On Tuesday he ate a hearty breakfast, and,
after breakfast, lay down and died.  A little lad lay on his
mat poorly.  " Father," he said, " what day is it to-day ?"
" Wednesday ! "  " Oh, well," he said, "on what day shall I
die ? I would like to die on Sunday."  When Sunday morning
came, he appeared better, and likely to recover.  " Father,"
he said, " what day is it to-day ?"  "Sunday ! "  "Oh, father,

I shall go to-day. When the sun is at the full I shall pass away." And so he did—died on Sunday at noon. A woman in a distant village sent for a teacher, to see her, as she felt she must die. She waited until the teacher arrived, received his sympathy and offices, and directly died.

An old man expected his son to come back from a journey. He fidgetted at his delay, stating that he was to die on Monday night ; but he must first see his son and say farewell. His son did not come on Monday, and so he said : " Well, he will be here to-morrow ; so I will wait and see him, and then die on Tuesday evening." His son did come ; he said farewell, and died on the Tuesday evening.

And these are not solitary cases. They seem to get an impression, and, unless very strong influences counteract, the impression acts so on the nervous system as even to destroy life. Just as the Frenchman, condemned to death, agreed to be bled to death in preference to dying at the hands of the executioner. He saw an array of surgical instruments, was then blindfolded, scratched on the arm, and water allowed, in imitation of blood, to trickle over the limb, faster and freer, until the poor victim sank in death—life destroyed or unhinged by nerve influences. And so with these children of nature—all the South Sea and Australasian aboriginals. But whence do they receive the impressions. The presence, in his garden or camp, of a certain plant said to be a death scavenger, has been known to cause the death of the unfortunate finder. Death-struck—bewitched—frightened out of existence.

The mind of a Fijian is highly philosophical. It is so in two aspects—the argumentative and the deductive.

He is pre-eminently a child of Nature. His communings are with Nature. He learns from Nature. He copies Nature. He knows almost every wild flower of his district, and can tell the stranger where each kind grows. He has studied their uses. From some he obtains his food, which is chiefly vegetable. From some he obtains his material for clothing, for rope and twine for fishing and other nets, and for all his primitive requirements. Among them he discovers his angona, wherewith to cheer and delight his heart, and he finds medicines for the various diseases to which he is subject. In argument, he draws his lessons from Nature's pictures. Speaking of a profession of Christianity, one of them compared a noisy and open profession to a mountain torrent. The still undemonstrative profession, he compared to the silent spring. Now, he said, to speak a fable, "The spring, which poured forth silently, complained to the mountain torrent about the great noise it made. See, said the spring, I go quietly on my course, carrying water to the sea ; but you spend your strength largely in roaring, foaming, hissing, and dashing among the rocks." And so the spring remonstrated, and many agreed that so much noise and show was not good. But, by-and-bye there came a long drought, and then the spring was dried up ; but the mountain torrent still rolled on. The silence of the spring proved its feebleness. It was not noisy in its flow because it had not the volumes of water; and hence, when the drought came, it soon dried up. So, he said, it is with religion. If a person have a great volume, he must be expressive and demonstrative. He must be seen and heard. But if there be not much religion in his breast, there is no volume to demonstrate, and so the flow is still; and when adversity and trial, as drought come, then his soul dries up.

Their public addresses—religious or otherwise—their tribal and other debates, are all illustrated by the same lines—the pencillings of Nature. And, from these, the speakers draw analogies or impress lessons.

The Fijians are highly artistic. They take great pains with their hair, and, on special occasions, that of a chief will be got up in the most artistic fashion. They adorn it most tastefully with flowers and ferns. They plant the most beautiful flowers in their gardens and around their homesteads. The various species of hibiscus do not appear to be indigenous, at all events to the southern Fijis, as they are never found wild. They are always and only found in inhabited or deserted villages; and it is a puzzle as to where and how they obtained them generations ago. Some are found in Asia, others in New Guinea. Did the Fijians obtain them thence? Ferns are often planted, and grow over the entrances of their houses. Their churches are often neatly decorated with cowry shells and other ornaments. Of old, their clubs and spears were elaborately and curiously carved, and that with tools the most meagre and primitive. Neat patterns are printed on

their native cloth, and pretty, though simple, designs on
their rude pottery.

Necessity is the mother of invention, and Nature is
the uncivilised people's great teacher. Hence, in the
cultivation of ndalo (together with yams, their staff of
life), the Fijians note that it requires for growth, good
alluvial soil, continuous wet, and plenty of air and room.
And so a native, where he cannot utilise natural swamps,
will search the mountain stream until he finds a portion
of the bank where he can, by means of small boulders and
stones from the brook, build a series of terraces, over
which a portion of the waters may slowly trickle. With
great care and neatness he builds up these terraces, finish-
ing with small stones, and capable of retaining a necessary
proportion of rich soil. And, at a proper distance apart, he
plants his ndalo roots, from which, in due course, he
obtains an abundant harvest. And furthermore, he learns
the wisdom of giving the ground a rest, and so shifts the
scene of his operations, and periodically chooses new
gardens.

I saw some wide moats, which reminded one of the old
Britons of two thousand years ago. It appears that these
were dug out as defence works. They were fairly wide,
deep, and for some three or four feet filled with mud and
shallow water. In this mud were implanted stakes, with
their sharp ends upwards, and so thickly together, as to
leave no room for stepping between. I had always been
led to believe that the ancient British moats were filled with
water, but on seeing the Fijian, the question arises, was

that feasible? The enemy, or a large proportion, could easily swim across such a narrow obstruction; but they could not cross, and especially with naked feet, a plantation of sharp stakes, spikes upward, and hidden and rendered more slippery and disagreeable by a thickness of soft mud and shallow water.

We have seen that the professed policy of the Government is to preserve the native race. This object is most noble and christianlike, if it be really intended. But actions speak louder than words; and, from the acts of the Government, only two inferences can be drawn— either that the expressed policy is a mere blind, or that the governing body is not competent to carry out its own programme.

We have endeavoured to show that the patriarchal government is deterrent to a people's advancement, and, in fact, to a people's civilization. It destroys the individual manhood, by rooting out the very foundations of independence, liberty, ambition, and wealth. And yet, the Government who profess such a vast anxiety for the preservation and protection of the natives, frames stringent laws for the maintenance of the patriarchal rule. And this rule is, in some respects, under the new *regime*, more grinding than under their own old tribal sway. There were, in the olden times, some restraints on the powers of a chief. He could—excepting as in Thakombau's or similar cases, where, by extra tribal and other means, he had obtained a more than solid footing —be at any time clubbed; or his people could leave him and go and join another tribe. But now the

English, as if afraid of an independent or straightforward policy, raise the chiefs and sub-chiefs and crush the people. They have the old power retained to them, and fortified by the backing of the British Lion. They can crush their people, and, though there may be nominal redress, yet red tapeism renders it of little or no effect. A native, if he feels himself aggrieved, has to come before the British Government through the very chief by whom he is aggrieved. And justice then is very tardy, or not forthcoming at all. It seems as if the chiefs kept the Government in fear; or it may be that the chiefs are pampered so as to save the trouble of dealing directly with the people.

A company wants 200 men. It opens relations with the chief and the Government; and the 200 men, as slaves, have to go, leaving wives and homes, whether they will it or no.

A man fell in love with a girl—a rare thing in Fiji, where marriages are arranged by the friends. He had to go to the lieutenant of the town—a petty sub-chief, and had to pay a trifle to get the application registered, and, if there were no lawful objection, the marriage licensed. The lieutenant, at the instance of a higher chief, refused the license. There was no lawful objection; but the chief either fancied the woman himself (a chief may have more wives than one), or he had a grudge against the poor man. Amazed, and at a loss to guess the reason, the man wrote to the chief, asking why he should interfere, and to allow him what was his rightful due—the license. The chief, in anger, had him seized and sent to a town some miles away as a prisoner. After a time, the man returned home. On re-entering the village, he was again seized by the chief and kept a prisoner—the chief saying the man was in his jurisdiction, and not under that of the English Government. The Government were communicated with, but they took no action. Slavery! Could anything be more vile; and the man a peaceable British subject. Is it come to this, after our glorious fights for freedom, that our Gracious Queen has to rule over slaves? And yet this feeble British Government allowed the man to be kept a prisoner by a petty powerful, impudent chief.

Slaves! Yes, the people are slaves. Lest the white man should put upon them, they are not allowed to work of their own free will. They belong to the patriarch or chief, who must not be offended ; and so, if they desire work, or if planters or others wish to hire labour, they must go to the chief or slave-holder. The law states that if a native wish to work, he must register his name on a public notice list ; he must obtain the consent of his tribal chief ; and he must obtain the consent of the Government. What a vast red tapeism, and need it be wondered, that it is a barrier, almost impenetrable, to the unsophisticated native.

But the man is to his town chief and tribal chief, property, and what is to compensate them for the loss sustained, for the time he may be away. The planter need to make this right by a bribe or present. Supposing all these preliminaries, after many delays and repeated official rebuffs, be surmounted, then the man goes for a certain wage and for a brief period only. It may be a month, three months, six months, or even a year, according to circumstances. If, out of his own district, further formalities have to be met, the man has to go before a magistrate, and various difficulties and obstructions have to be removed. After doing his term of service, he may engage again, provided the gauntlet be run as before. And, after all this toil and working, he has to give a portion—at the lowest, one-tenth—of his wages to the chief, and submit to the begging of his friends, for to rid himself of most of the remainder.

When desirous of taking a native canoe and a couple of men for a tour of the river, I had to apply to the chief of the town. He was very pompous, and stated that his desire was to assist me, but he could not spare the time that day; he would see to it on the morrow. A secretary, who was writing letters to the council of chiefs, then sitting, said to him: "We must make commission out of this." "No," he said. "This man is a doctor of medicine. He has not come to buy or to sell: but he has come to study science. We know nothing of science, and he wants to find out the cure for diseases, and how to benefit us. You shall not make anything out of him. He shall pay the two men one shilling a day each and rations, and I myself will lend him a canoe. I thought I had certainly got hold of a most sensible and hospitable chief, and shook hands with him most cordially. Next day he spent the morning in getting the boys and the canoe, and we at length started. The boys were everything that could be wished. They worked willingly; they climbed trees of their own accord whenever they sighted a new plant or fern; they took the

greatest care of my belongings ; they explained as well as
possible by signs, places, and matters of interest ; warned
me of dangers, and assisted generally in the collecting of
natural history objects. They appeared happy and free,
chatting merrily, and laughing and singing the whole day
long.

On my return, after eleven days' absence, I paid each of
them the sum agreed upon, and made each of them a present of tobacco for general good behaviour and assistance.
Next day the chief, with several attendants, visited me.
They had blackened their faces, and endeavoured to make
their visages look terrible. I was informed by an interpreter that the chief wanted the money for the boys and
the boat. I answered that I had paid the boys themselves.
" No ! No ! You were to pay the chief. The bargain
was with him. He gave you the boys. And, moreover, he wants ten shillings for the loan of the boat." I
explained that such an item was never mentioned, and the
alleged reason of the chief's liberality. Remonstrance was
useless. The interpreter then stated that the chief would
send for his policemen and have me arrested. On hearing
this, my anger was fairly aroused, and I told him, in
satire, to duck himself in the river—so contemptible
did I consider his double-dealing. The whole affair
ended in the boys coming forward with the money, and in
my having to pay the ten shillings for the boat. Two days
afterwards, this same chief came and endeavored to excuse
himself, blaming misunderstandings to the interpreter.
After a time, putting his hand over his heart, he said : " I
cannot be right until we become friends, and shake hands ;

and so I had to forgive and be friends ; glad to find, even in this man, who was everywhere spoken of as a villain, some effects of missionary example and teaching. As it was, the matter was legally entirely against me. I had not been used in free England, or in equally free Victoria, to pay the slave-holder, and so I made a mistake, and paid the let-out-on-hire slaves. And I was really liable by English law, and could have been sued to Suva, the capital, and made to pay the chief, the full amount due for both boys. These latter, influenced by missionary teaching, got me out of the difficulty by paying the chief themselves. But how galling—paying the price of their own labour, and trusting, if perhaps they might have a moiety returned. And this law is administered so as to protect and preserve the native race ! Truly, protect them from drinking the sweets of liberty : preserve them intact, in body and estate, to their hereditary holders.

The following practically proves the power of the chiefs, and the position of the English Government :—A chief, wishing to obtain an object of value, levied a contribution from his people of ten shillings per head. The levy was paid. Soon afterwards he saw a fine boat, upon which he also set his heart. He sent round to demand another ten shillings levy. One of the towns was too poor to pay this levy. They waited upon him, and stated that they could not pay. He appeared to accept their excuse. Shortly afterwards, an application was made to him for labour. He sent the men from the offending town. On the completion of the work, the chief received the payment in full. The men, on their return, applied to him for their share.

He only laughed at them, and reminded them that they would not pay the ten shillings levy, and so now he had paid it for them. Aggrieved, the men appealed to the English Government ; but this milk-and-water body was too timid or too cautious to interfere. Moreover the Government officials aided the political leaders, by having the news of the complaint lodged, made known to the chief. He immediately acted with promptness, and had the offenders arrested. They were sent to a distant town, and detained for some three months. An English philanthropist let it be known to the chief, that if the men were not released, he would openly fight the Government on their behalf, and so they were released. But alas, for the stain on the British flag, that outrage on British subjects has never been righted or avenged. Justice has been withheld. And in numbers of other and similar instances, England's flag of liberty has thus been trodden under foot by these feeble representatives of the British crown.

The Government affirm that the Fijians would not be satisfied unless governed by their own chiefs. Why, then, did they ask to be annexed under the British Throne? If the Fijian chiefs are to govern Fiji on the patriarchal system, then what necessity is there for England to govern as a Crown colony? What absurdity to run two lines of Government, and so diametrically opposite, at one and the same time ! The policy of the Government states, we must make laws to preserve the natives intact, and to protect them from the designings of the whites. Glorious philanthropy ! Worthy the highest commendation ! *But does it protect or preserve* ? It throws around them a cloak of preservation and protection, but what are the destructive and deadly agencies which are concealed within! The people, before a superior race, do need protection to hold their own. And judged from the past, and from the various developments of the slave trade, they need protection against intrigue and villany on the part of some of the whites. For again and again, unprincipled, selfish whites have, by bribes and promises in times past, got and retained natives wrongly. But it is the height of folly, in seeking to avoid an evil, to fly from one extreme to the other. In protecting a man from the oppressor, do not rob him of his liberty by yourself manacling his chains. Yet this is practically what the English Government are doing. In protecting the Fijians, they cut off liberty and make voluntary labour a non-potest. If I want a servant, I must get the permission of chiefs, sometimes townships, and friends, and Government. And so, if a Fijian is anxious to come into my employ, he must obtain the same permission.

It is urged in favour of the Government policy, that the drafting men off to plantations and mills would depopulate the native villages, and thus at once scatter the people and prevent their natural increase. But is this theory valid? At present, in many villages, the women largely do the field labour. The men may assist at times; but, for the most part, they take things easy. Again, a very few weeks in the year are sufficient for all purposes of agriculture. Their food is simple; their wants are few; and, at present, a large number of men are often away for days or weeks together, let out on hire by their chiefs; also on the

Government lands, farming out the native taxes. But why is it indispensable that the survivorship of the people should be dependent on the maintenance of the patriarchal bondage. The natives cannot rise under such a bondage, since individuality is crushed in the communal. And, if this weaker race cannot rise, before and in the presence of a superior race, *they must* in time *become extinct.* It is thus the sheerest folly to imagine that patriarchal rule and communal life, on present village sites, are absolutely necessary to the protection and preservation of the race. If such really were the case, then the Government would be sacrificing the people, in allowing as they do, such a number to leave for longer or shorter periods. Their own actions in this matter belie their announced belief. But is it necessary that the free and righteous service of the men, further from or nearer to their homes, should really destroy their social and family life ? At the present, the people are decreasing in numbers. Many foolish laws prevent the increase of population. A man is so restricted in marriage choice. He has to get so many people to consent. Marriage is, with rare exceptions, simply an alliance planned out by relations, or by the tribe. And, altogether, there is a growing disinclination to marriage on the part of the male population. The women also, as a rule, object to the trouble of many children. Wives will often leave their husbands for months, or even years. Abortion is freely practised, and not scientifically : but in such a manner as to damage and make prematurely old the constitution and health. Diseases introduced by the whites and labour boys have, and are still, lessening the

numbers. And so we see really that village life does not
keep up the population. I was informed in official circles
that about 7000 able-bodied males were hired out to work.
How many of these are married? Are not the greater
number practically living as unmarried? For where is the
family life to such as are married, while the husbands are
on the plantation, if the wives and children remain in the
distant township. The great remedy is that already the
right of the Fijians—personal freedom. Will freedom then
decimate the numbers? If a man be free to engage his
services, in any plantation or homestead distant or near to
his own township, need that prevent his family life? If
the law have any power or supervision at all for the protection of the native race, would it not be wiser in all ways
to enact that the Fijian, as a free man, might engage
himself as a labourer: but that it be essential for him to
take with him a wife, and that such couple be provided
with hut, and allowed a portion of land on which to culti-
vate their necessary vegetable provisions. It is not the
village, but the individual, married life which enlarges a
nation. Thus, marriage and individual exertions would
be encouraged. But, as it is at present, married life is
discouraged, and all parties discontented.

The labour traffic has for some time occupied the
attention of the British nation. It is nothing more nor
less than a veritable British slave trade. What means the
old song,

"Britons never shall be slaves."

Where is all the glory of British liberty, battled for and
obtained by Wilberforce, Buxton, and a host of others?"

Where is the brightness and grandeur of the British flag, which the Queen of the Seas displayed before all nations and peoples. " Destruction to slavery and to the slave trade for ever." Who are those who stand in the places of the heroes of the past, and who fear to speak out the national watchword, " England and liberty?" Is there no national honour left ? Is England to be cowed by any and every opposing nation, while she herself descends to imbrue her hands in the shed blood of the accursed slave traffic ? Rise up ye spirits of the departed and weep for your sons ! Lament ye sages, for England is once more a slave-holding nation !

The reasons which have led to this are the desire of aspiring British subjects to possess large estates, and the difficulty of making those estates pay, excepting by working them at a labour price low enough, to allow competition with similar estates and industries in other countries.

It is urged that Europeans cannot work in the open air, and in the sugar-fields of the South Pacific Islands. And, moreover, competition is so great that it is asserted the sugar industry could not be carried on in Fiji or even in Queensland, if current wages, as obtained among Europeans, had to be paid. The planters cry out : " We *must have* labour, and we must have cheap labour. We have vested interests." Thus the labour industry, as European, is effectually closed. The climatic influences, as against such a labour in Fiji, are very greatly exaggerated. The temperature averages 70 to 80 degrees for several months in the year, and up to 85 or 86 degrees, occasionally reaching 90 degrees in the other months. The nights, in most parts of the group, are cooled by sea breezes. The rainfall varies. At Suva, the capital, it averages 110 inches per annum; while up the Rewa, in the sugar country, it even in one part reaches 190 inches. Now the heat is greatly below that of Australia in the summer, and there is not the cold of Australia in the winter. The rainfall is largely during night, and the sun soon dries the vegetation. Even in Fiji, English mechanics, as carpenters, boat-builders, and others, work hard for long hours, and out of doors, and yet enjoy very good health. English overseers, and others in authority, have to superintend the labour in the fields, and yet suffer little in consequence. The men in the English ironworks and foundries have to work harder, and to be exposed to a far higher heat. They have likewise to be subjected to the dust and fumes, occasioned from their work. They have not the fresh island air to restore lost vigour; and they are unavoidably subjected to sudden changes of temperature, especially in the outside chills of an English winter. And provided that caution were exercised as to the hours and time for cleaning the canes, which would require a comparative small percentage of the whole time and labour, doubtless Europeans could be employed. In England, agricultural labourers used to get only nine shillings a week; they can now obtain twelve to fifteen shillings, and, if the proprietors of plantations and sugar-mills can pay the black man or coolie two shillings a day, he could probably, with equal profit, pay an industrious Englishman, who would do double the work, four shillings per diem. But whether or not this might be effected, and thousands of the half-starving Londoners be thus provided for, it has not been done ; and the cry has been urged, " We must have cheap labour."

As noted before, the Fijians are averse to working on their own lands, and for foreigners. And further, having always led an easy life, unless they want to obtain some commodity, they do not care to work at all. This, no doubt, in past years led to many irregularities, the white people thinking it essential to their interests to obtain Fijian servants, and thus, by stratagem, obtaining and detaining such service. And so the English Government stepped in and interfered, but, in legislating, went to the other extreme, thus damaging both white man and black. They, in seeking to prevent irregularities on the part of the whites, put an almost effectual barrier against the employment of Fijians, excepting as slaves lent out by their chiefs, and that with circumscribed restrictions.

No doubt, as it is now, the larger number of white people having a stake in the country, would, if it were in their power, force the Fijians to perform the necessary manual and menial labour. This would be highly wrong. These natives have land, they have food, and their wants are few ; and white men have no right to consider them as property, or bond-slaves, or servants. Service should certainly be encouraged ; but service under a patriarchal bondage is not service, but slavery. The patriarchal rule should be sapped, and then each man, as a free, independent British subject, should be encouraged to do something. But, as it is now, the Fijian revolts against work, which is

to him of little vantage. And it is only because his mental
capacities are not awakened into the keen-sightedness of
Englishmen, that in any case he submits to work at all.
And thus the whites, judging the natives as lazy and
repugnant to work, and seeing their own interests suffering in consequence, condemn him most severely; and too
many treat him as a dog, and not as a brother.

The Fijian Government, and, through them, the English
Government, have legalised the labour traffic. Queensland
also has taken her share in the same. Certain regulations
are enacted, ostensibly to prevent irregularities, and to give
the traffic an air of respectability. But those who make
the regulations have not the power to enforce, only in part:
and they have not the means or the power to regulate
matters in the land of purchase, and even on the voyage.

To form a correct judgment as to the righteousness of
the traffic, I will make a comparison between the old slave
trade and this legalised labour traffic :—

SLAVE TRADE PRACTICES.

1. Coast tribes by war or kidnapping, obtained people
from inland tribes.

2. These were sold as slaves.

3. They were overcrowded in
vessels with inferior accommodation.

LABOR TRAFFIC CUSTOMS.

1. Coast tribes, by war or kidnapping, obtain men from
inland tribes. The whites
also buy and otherwise en-
tice unsuspecting victims
by promises and bribes.

2. These are sold to the labour
vessels, If they refuse to
go on board, the coast
people club and eat them.

3. By regulation, only a certain
number are allowed on
each vessel.

4. They had to be chained or otherwise watched and guarded on the voyage.

4. The boys, as they are called, have to be watched; so many allowed on deck at a time; the hatches guarded at night by men with revolvers, and other precautionary measures adopted.

5. Many died on the voyage.

5. A high percentage, considering the time and numbers shipped, die on the voyage.

6. They were knocked down to the highest bidder, to do work on plantations, or for domestic use.

6. They used to be handed over to ready-money buyers; but now Government appoints them, securing a year's wages, nominally so called, beforehand.

7. Many died at an early period, on the plantations, from grief, work, hardships, and resulting diseases.

7. Many die soon after arrival on the plantations. Oftentimes, and especially in Queensland, the mortality is frightfully high.

8. Families were torn asunder; but, if it suited the master, family life was encouraged, and children brought up on the estate.

8. Family life is not encouraged. The boys are shipped alone, very few women and no children accompanying the men.

9. As far as practicable, it was to the interest of the slave-owner to feed his slaves and to treat them well—the more healthy the slaves, the more the amount of work to be got out of them.

9. It is the policy for the planter to feed and treat the labour boys well.

10. If the slaves quarrelled and fought, the master or overseer took the authorative, and chastised the culprits.

10. If the boys are refractory or if they quarrel, there is redress to be had by law; but oftentimes it becomes almost imperative to use timely physical force, and otherwise to punish the offenders.

11. The slaves were free to rove over the estate: but were not permitted to leave it, excepting on plantation business and with proper precautions.

11. The labour boys are free; but are practically prisoners in the island to which they are shipped.

12. The service demanded from them was manual or domestic.

12. The services demanded are manual and domestic.

13. The black slave was looked down upon by the whites as an inferior being, and was often snubbed and treated discourteously.

13. The labour boy is looked down upon. He is not respected, and is too often snubbed, and ordered about with oaths and threats.

14. Oftentimes, in the capture of slaves, blood was shed.

14. Often, in the obtaining of boys, blood is shed.

15. Oftentimes the vessels were unseaworthy.

15. Oftentimes the vessels have been, and even are now, unseaworthy.

To review the above—

1 & 2. The recognized rule among the labour vessels is, so to speak, to pay a bounty, and practically to bribe or to beguile the unsuspecting natives into selling their own liberty.

If they do not sell themselves, the chiefs are tempted

by the offer of muskets, tobacco, &c., to press young men into the service.

But with labour vessels visiting the islands, the coast tribes soon find it to their interest to obtain slaves or prisoners of war and to give them in exchange for the bounty.

The South Sea Islanders are in mental capacities and development only on a par with the Fijian, and with the English schoolboy. They look but to the hour. The possession of a musket and a knife, and the promises of vast gifts in the future, and too often of a Paradise of fabricated luxuries lure them on their doom. People speak of this as a *bona fide* engagement! What ludicrous nonsense! The savage, free from labour and toil, suddenly becomes wise and loving, and offers for a paltry pittance to carry his life in his hands ; to work hard in the interests of the white man ; and to resign his liberty for a period! Wonderful phenomenom. And so anxious is he, that he is ready to leave his home and friends for a period of years, and to trust to strangers for means of return. And if they cannot brace themselves up to the ordeal, the tribe, valueing the opportunities given, bring chieftain and tribal influences to bear, and so compel the young men thus to raise and improve themselves. How discerning, these savage islanders! Just as the simple English country girl in London, in the hands of a sharper, appreciates her position and the advantages to be obtained, and so knowingly rushes into the snares awaiting her! The little ones went willingly! And so may the savages. But neither have the experience nor intelligence to judge of their doings. They simply are enticed by the sweets. But oftener than not, these savages, as too often happens to little children, have their liberty yielded up for them. In one instance, as an example, I heard of four boys being purchased from a chief for four rifles. And only last year a vessel was dismissed the trade because it was discovered that the pay was to depend on the numbers obtained.

3. If fortunate enough to obtain as many, 150 to 200 are packed or stowed away in a schooner of 150 tons. They are kept in large bunks, several in a bunk, and in the pitching and tossing of the vessel, fall into rough usage through falling on, and rolling over each other. These vessels are often abominably dirty, unhealthy and unseaworthy, but such before coming into port are thoroughly cleaned and renovated—the hold is white-washed, probably fresh paint is utilized, and a thorough scouring is administered. A clean ship, a good meal, often a champagne festival awaits the Government official —and on his passing his word—the scheming has succeeded and the men are ready for moneyed applicants.

4. As must be easily imagined in such a nefarious traffic, the victims have to be guarded. It is not safe to allow many on deck at a time. Men are ready armed to subdue a rush, if such be attempted, or to prevent escape, if any seek to jump overboard and swim ashore. In properly fitted vessels, on either side of the hatchway is a large slab of iron and wood, which can be made to fall down and effectually stop the hatchways. Two men with revolvers need always to be on the alert to insure the safety of the crew. The hatchways also have to be

specially guarded at night. In fact, how can it be otherwise? The victims probably rendered more irritable by sea sickness, rolling and pitching, and goaded by the defensive precautions of the crew, and after reflection filled with remorse at leaving home, friends, and fatherland, would avail themselves of any opportunity which offered for revenge or escape. It must not for a moment be supposed that the labour boys are a group of happy, contented lads, bent on a voyage of discovery and fortune-seeking. Such ambition does not trouble the patriarchal-governed savage. The majority of the boys are sold by others, or are nefariously entrapped, bribed by a present bounty, and lured by promise of future rewards. And most of them, when on board, would most gladly flee to their own native shores. And hence, as it is to the invested interests of the labour hunters to retain them, there are two opposing interests. Moral suasion would be comparatively feeble under such circumstances. Might must maintain its rights, be those rights ever so unjust. Where so many boys are shipped, and from so many different villages, old feuds and fresh quarrels often lead to squabbles and bloodshed; and cases have come to light where the crew have had to use fire-arms to enforce order and to secure the public safety. In fact, looked at in all its bearings, it would not be either safe or expedient for the labour crew to carry so many, slaves, and savages, unguarded. And it has been asserted, and no doubt is correct, that in many instances the most refractory have had to be thrown into irons, and often, as a precaution, on nearing their own islands. (Not much like a free and optional service!)

One young man, who was in the traffic for five years, told me for a positive fact, that the boys are kept almost, or entirely, naked during the voyage ; but on coming near the port of purchase, they are clothed, receiving a pair of trousers, a shirt, and a hat. They are generally fed well on yams, taro, and cocoa-nuts, with every other day an allowance of salt beef. Only during July of this year, a labour vessel was seized by a British man-of-war, when a number of the boys jumped overboard and swam for the shore. What was it that prevented their doing so before, unless the application of force ?

5-7. Many die. The Fiji Government report of this year says : " The number of Polynesian immigrants introduced from the first day of January, 1878, to the last day of December, 1881, into the colony is 7,137. There died out of this number, during the above period, 1,270 souls, who had been passed by the medical inspector as fit for indenture. The death-rate on shipboard in 1878 was set down at 9·3 per centum : and this, most probably, was under the mark ; so given for purposes of policy on the part of interested parties. In 1879 the rate was again high, ten dying in one ship while at sea, and 56 in the hospital after landing. The rate was somewhat lower in 1882 and 1883. In Suva hospital, containing 26 beds, the death-rate in 1882 was 235·53 per mille. Out of an estimate of 5,979 men, 603 deaths occurred, or 108·06 per mille. In five plantations, employing 554 men, 264 died. And further statistics show that where few men are allotted, the death-rate is considerably lower than on the large estates ; thus proving that on these large estates many are lost who, if

they had had the care and attention given to the few, by
small planters and others, would have recovered. On the
Colonial Sugar Company's three Rewa plantations,
employing some 471, some 240, or over 50 per cent., died.
And it is for to develop this sugar industry that Polynesian labour has been imported. The boys from some
districts, notably New Britain and other parts, die off in
very large numbers. The percentage is largely dependent
on the native habitat of the boys, on the character of such
habitat, on the former manner of life, on the varieties of
food used, on the habits generally, on the climatic influences, on the moral sensibilities. It is also influenced by
the character and hardships of the work imposed, by the
treatment of overseers and others, and by the character
and influence of individuals with whom the labourers come
to be associated.

One gentleman, partner in one of the large companies,
assured me that he could not account for the heavy death-
rate. Referring to the comparing the labour traffic to the
slave-trade, he quoted as instance of what might be mag-
nified into brutality, the treatment of the sick. Many of
the attacked, under fits of desperation, or during the deli-
rium of fever, become very violent, and have to be bound
by force. Such, he remarked, might be construed into
slave-trade oppression, whereas it is for the poor fellows'
*own good*, and for the safety of all the plantation hands.

Another gentleman, and one disinterested in the traffic,
explained as one reason of a high death rate in some plantations, the failure of the overseer to discriminate between
illness and sulkiness. And hence, too often the sick boys

are kept at work, or out in the field too long. And thus, when really admitted for medical treatment, the case is hopelessly incurable. Another reason is probably the fear of the Government to allow fires at night. The Fijians are most sensitive to the cold, and very often sleep with their backs to a big fire. Natives from islands nearer the Equator must feel the lowered temperature of the nights, and doubtless not being allowed to keep fires through the night, and not being clothed, get chills, and thus lay the foundation of various diseases.

Change of food, eating unripe fruit. and probably the free drinking of water when hot, are causes which induce dysentery, a disease too often fatal. But again, the medical aid is sadly defective and inadequate. Ten medical men are provided by Government for all the Fijis. These are mostly young men of little experience, and who have a small salary for a heavy amount of work. There is no keen competition for success and fame. It does not pay to give each case the most careful daily attention. And further, the villages and plantations are too distant from each other to admit of proper attention. While I was in Fiji, the hooping cough was very prevalent. At one large township, the doctor arrived after a few day's notification. A mixture was ordered, but the Fijians had no faith in the doctor or the physic. He was too distant in manner, and had failed too often in practice to secure their respect or trust. Hence they had recourse to their own remedies, but being a new disease, it baffled them, and the children died by scores. One day I heard a most strange noise in the middle of the river, and on looking, perceived that it was

made by children, who came up to the surface (they were
diving and swimming) to cough. The doctor's visit over,
and his *duty* performed, he left for a township further on.
And this besides his regular plantation work. And so the
comparatively unattended children died by hundreds. It
may be urged, as arguments of the gentlemen before
alluded to prove, that the labour boys have to suffer through
force of circumstances. But where is the right to make
them suffer these things. What is the reason—the inducement—the first cause which brings about all these
circumstances which lead to all this suffering. Far better
answered one gentleman, "to be in a civilized country than
killing and eating each other." So argued the old slave
holders and traffickers. " Far better to be in Christian
homesteads than in heathen darkness." But is the remedy
any better than the disease ? And what power or
authority does the white man claim for applying the
remedy ! Is it not simply a matter of amassing wealth,
through these poor savages, by caprice, force and cunning!
How far would one of these professed humanitarians move
in the matter if it were not for personal profit ? Who are
these savages, and of what use in the world, lazy dogs and
cumberers of the ground ?

> Dogs they are—dogs, and nothing more ?
> No soul to love, no spirit to adore !
> But fit for slaves, as slaves they were at first ;
> No mind to ken, though kicked, and cuffed, and cursed !
> Depravity ! Well may the angels weep.
> And sons of men in dust and ashes keep :
> While He, who counts the sparrows as they fall,
> In vengeance waits to hear each feeble call.

8. In the old slave trade, one redeeming feature, and which really led to the eventual elevation and improvement of the negro race, was the permitted, and, to a degree, protected, family life. But in Polynesian labour traffic, family life is destroyed. During one period of immigration, as calculated, 18 women were imported to between five and six thousand men: and the full average proportion was a little over 9 per cent., as women to men. This, of course, is damaging to the races, and damaging to the morals. And thus, under this heading, the old slave trade was really less baneful than the labour traffic. It may be urged, in palliation, that the men chosen are mostly young, and that at the end of three years, they are free to return. But they are often induced to repeat the term of service, and so to pass the flower of their existence away from their kindred, and alone.

9. No doubt, many stay a second term of service because they are well fed and fairly well treated. Many also fear the return voyage, and their reception in their native land. If landed away from their own villages, they are often killed and eaten, and as they are not always adepts at remembering the way by sea to their own parts, or as it may not suit captains to lengthen the voyage, this sometimes happens, and it is certainly not inviting to be returned to a stranger village as provender. Again, doubtless, many remain because they do not like the warlike life they have to lead at home, and because, on the whole, they really prefer life as labour boys. At one house, where I was staying, was a boy of this class. He was naturally thoughtful. He was a native of the Solomon Islands. He

was a useful and quiet servant, rarely needing to be told a second time. One day he was sent with me to assist in collecting. As soon as I had succeeded in showing what and how to collect, he displayed great acumen and diligence, and found a large number and variety of specimens. He could not stand chaff—the Fijians and other Polynesians, chaffed him as they passed, I presume on his position as labour boy. He showed great agitation at times, and, at last, put down his load and gave chase to three or four Fijian youths who had impudently saluted him. On ;the next Sunday, he was one of fifteen Solomon Islanders who had a hand to hand fight, the cause of the quarrel being over a woman. The police stepped in, and gave this poor fellow two months' imprisonment. Speaking some time before about a native meke or dance. he stated his views ; that such was folly and waste of time ; that it needed long practice to prepare, and did no good when given. And this man a heathen, and, before captured by the labour vessel, a great warrior. And to avoid the troubles of warfare, and the follies or waste of time, as he styled it, over other heathen customs, he re-engaged for a second term of service. His mate and special friend, who had also engaged for a second period, was even more quiet and docile, not having such a hasty temper. Both of these boys only needed the elevating influences of the gospel of Christianity to make them thoroughly good, useful members of society, and to civilization. But although, on the whole, labour boys are well-treated, the term must be qualified. A farmer treats his horses, and cattle, and dogs well if he feed them well, leave no

scars on the hide, and do not work them to death. But many
may be the blows dealt to the horse—many the kicks
applied to the dog. Yet, on the whole, they are treated
well. And so the Polynesians and Fijians may, in like
manner, and doubtless are, on the whole, well treated.

According to the *Argus* issue of July 5th, 1884, the
Agent-General of Fiji says :—"Assaults on the persons
of Polynesians are very numerous, and should be firmly
discountenanced, especially in cases of new immigrants,
with whom apparent idleness or stupidity may frequently
be the result of weakness or disease. I have little doubt,
from my experience of Polynesians, that death, in
the case of more than one immigrant, has been greatly
accelerated by assaults; though it would be most difficult
to produce sufficient evidence to secure a conviction for
manslaughter, the effects produced being exhibited rather
in the form of mental despondency than actual bodily
injury." There is law for the Polynesian ; yet, since there is
so much formality as too often to deter a white man from
having resort thereto, how is it any wonder that the difficulties deter savages, and especially savages who do not
comprehend or understand its meaning or provisions. But
with this drawback, in 1882 forty-eight complaints were
lodged against employers, resulting in 38 convictions. And
these, by savages against nominal Christians and civilized
men ! As stated before, one of my first sights in Fiji, on landing was to see a Government official kick a Fijian. The
official had on light, soft boots, and so left no mark for the
law to lay hold of him. But there is a form of insult
which the Polynesian feels more severely than physical

torture, and that is cold and indifferent treatment, satire, and calumny. And here the law, speaking generally, cannot interfere. A master may treat his labour boy as a dog, and treat him well physically, but yet treat him badly in a moral sense. And speaking generally, the master does not seek to elevate his men, either by bringing them under the influences of Christianity, elementary education, or otherwise. All he wants is the largest amount of manual labour out of them ; and, too often, he not only sets an example of selfishness, but also of gross immorality.

10. Often, on board ship, the boys of tribes at variance, or even boys of the same tribe or township quarrel ; and at times force has to be used to quell the disturbance. And, on the plantations, disputes must naturally frequently arise. The quarrelling parties oftentimes fall back on their old tactics, and threaten to use knives or other instruments to hand. One overseer told me he had had to put down such disturbances by force, and by threatening firearms. One man he had to cow by felling him to the ground. In 1882 the masters brought forward 97 complaints against Polynesians, and the convictions were 57. But a single thought will show to the reflective mind the little likelihood, excepting in severe cases, of the masters troubling to appeal to the law. A cuff or gentle kick is often practically the more efficacious, and how can the offender appeal against this when he himself was the aggressor. Thus, there is a vast amount of the inner life of this sad traffic which is hidden from the world.

11. Not only are the labour boys detained, and kept practically prisoners until the expiration of their term of

service, but they are under continuous Government supervision ; and, at the expiration of their term, are not free
to live as they like. They must be subjected to a vast
amount of red-tapeism—again agree to a further term of
indenture, or be shipped back to their islands. And even
the Fijians, who, as British subjects, are by national tradition and rights free, cannot leave the islands of their own
free will and accord. If they want to leave, they must get
a European, with property, to be bound for them in the
sum of £50 or £100 for a period of six or twelve months,
when, if they wish a prolonged term, they must return to
Fiji and go through the same official overhauling as
before. Now, we can understand the fear of Government
lest ill-principled men should take these simple-minded
away people for selfish motives only. And we could understand a wise Government seeing it a duty to stop any
such emigration, if for the purpose of slavery or rapine.
But when a family who has treated a native well is willing, by the desire of that native, to take him as a servant
to Sydney or other Australian colonies, why make him
and treat him as a slave. In Sydney, and in Australia
generally, there is the protection of the law, and more
righteously than in Fiji. What, then, is there to fear in
allowing the native, of his own accord, visiting distant
lands.

12. The services demanded of the labour boys are
manual and domestic. Field labour is scarce—domestic
servants cannot be obtained ; and, if at all, at a high
figure. And so these poor savages, so called, are required

and pressed into service by the more powerful and knowing whites.

13. Many planters, and others employing native labor. will openly avow that these men are no higher than dogs ; and, as before stated, believing, or feigning to believe such, they treat them discourteously, and often badly. " See," say these men, " there is no gratitude in the blackfellow. He is a liar, thief, hypocrite, cheat. and villain." And, if true. then thankful, truthful. honest, straightforward, and respectable civilized white man could not respect such. But are these sweeping declamations true ? And is civilized man thankful, truthful, straightforward, and respectable?

As far as experience teaches, man all over the world is born in sin and shapen in iniquity The animal, or instinctive. is naturally selfish. And it is only philosophy which can raise him above these low degradations. And it is only the Christian philosophy which in any degree can purify his heart, as well as raise his moral tone and character. Now, the English have been trained in this philosophy for generations, and yet we see the most glaring vice, the most clever frauds and wholesale swindles, the most loathsome and debasing national drunkenness. Civilized society is one continuous struggle for the pre-eminence. Thousands make haste to be rich by grinding down their dependents and fellows. White lies, and especially in trade, are fashionable. And looking at the professing Christian community—those who, in their respective churches, profess to have turned their backs upon the world and its fashions—where are the consecrated millions for carrying the gospel to every nation, and people, and tongue? Where are the hundreds of thousands spent righteously in giving employment to, and in relieving the wants of, the poor, the destitute, and the sick, and in raising the people generally, socially, morally, and intellectually. So strong is the animal selfishness of man, that with rare exceptions, the Christianity of eighteen centuries has produced a race, who put a small coin on the collection plate, or who, after a sensational or emotional speech, may dole out a half-crown or a guinea in support of the grandest objects ever brought before their notice. The English owe everything to Christianity; and yet, how faults abound!

But turn to Fiji—behold Melanesia. Naturally sunken to murder and cannibalism and the lowest degradation! In the stone age. But Christianity comes in, and the Fijians and islanders where the glorious philosophy is carried, give up their murder and cannibalism. Some may still lie, some may cheat. The lying and cheating and thieving is most prevalent in the white settlements. This is acknowledged even by the police authorities. In my journey inland, I left my belongings loose in the canoe, and often unguarded, yet I lost nothing. But in the settlements, these children imitate bad white men. Nevertheless a very large proportion are seeking to obey the moral law. Look at the Sabbath in these islands of Polynesia, where the gospel has penetrated, a larger per centage of the black population keep the Sabbath, and worship in the sanctuary, than is the case with the white men. And in the matter of barter, these blacks are but

as children, only lately having any civilized ideas at all of
commercial relations and of relative value. And what an
example the white man sets! On my inland journey I
had to buy rations of biscuits. I received double the
number for my money, the furthest inland, and where the
item of carriage was vastly the heaviest. And repeatedly
as it is well known, the whites get a heavy price for poor
articles and give a mere nothing for valuable returns. In
one instance a man beginning with a bag of salt, and
bartering for yams, at length by trading, obtained hundreds
of pounds worth of curiosities and goods during his visits
to some hill tribes. And naturally the blacks, seeing that
the whites only look upon such dealings as smart business
tact, retaliate. And as they begin to understand the
value of things, and to recognise the commercial acumen,
they naturally seek to imitate. But as a whole, while in
Fiji, I found the dealings of the blacks more righteous,
and less grasping and unfair, than those of the whites.
In judging these children in intelligence, let him that is
without sin, cast the first stone. It is too often as a
gentleman proved in Fiji that those to complain are the
greatest sinners. A Chief was grumbling that the
Government had not discovered and punished a white
offender for assault and violence. But answered the white
man, they instituted enquiries and could not find the
criminal. Yes, he replied, we know all about it. It did
not suit them to find out. If it had been a black fellow,
he would soon have been discovered and punished. The
white men are only deceivers and liars. After further dis-
cussion and only likely to lead to high words or feelings,

the white man replied. When people live near and see
a bad example continuously before them, is it any wonder
that they copy and do likewise. Now if I lived here I
might imitate the bad example and should then become a
liar and a rogue. And what besides can you expect from
the whites, who you say have so acted, and who live so
close to yourself. The chief was noted as a black leg and
a scoundrel, and at once perceived the home thrust, and
with a loud laugh was glad to close the conversation.

As to the question of hypocrisy, levelled at the blacks,
who profess Christianity. In fair play, it should be remembered that these people have just emerged from the lowest
degradation. It should also be remembered as before
stated, that in intellect and mental capacities they
are on an average with the English public schoolboy.
Why then judge severely. I was once at a meeting of a
religious body, where there were some children, who had
professed sorrow for sin, and a desire to lead new lives. The
service was somewhat tiresome and heavy—and two or
three of these children began to play with a handkerchief,
folding it up as a doll and in other ways trifling and
forgetting the sanctity of the service. But shall I therefore at once damn these children ! Because they were
inexperienced and so not on their guard, and because the
flesh was weak and the intellectual faculties feeble, am 1
to say that those children had no desire to live a good
life ? Rise from this, a step higher, and compare self—
who never wanders in church—who is never frivilous—
who, in fact, has kept the moral law to the letter ! There

is none righteous—no, not one. But judge these Polynesians by the spirit of their intents and conduct, and in a very large percentage it will be found that they are often a pattern to more highly favoured nations. Their feebleness, as children, is against them. Like children, they often lack moral courage to stand satire, and too often, under the satire and bad example of the whites, they forget their religion, and backslide. And as to the charge of ingratitude : As mentioned before, the more refined passions are not perfected in children ; neither in Fijians. And the expression of the same in adult Europeans depends largely upon the constitutional temperament. Some are emotional and demonstrative ; others are philosophical and cold. Some are thoughtful and reflective ; others are flighty and superficial. But taking civilized and Christianized people all round, how often, comparatively speaking, do we find real gratitude ? Politeness and refined acknowledgment often give the lie to the feelings of the heart. And it still too frequently is, as it was eighteen centuries ago. Ten lepers were healed, and one returned to give thanks ; but where were the nine ? Let the philosopher look at the Fijian, then at the English public school-boy, and then at himself ; and let him who is blameless, ever thankful and righteous before God and man, blame and denunciate the Fijian.

14. Often, in this labour traffic, blood is shed. Numbers of cases never come to light, being, in the mutual interests of all concerned, hushed up.

One young man in the trade related to me an instance in point. He said : "I don't like the missionaries ; they are no good." Somewhat surprised, I asked why. "Because," he said, "I was in a boat's party, and we visited a distant part of the coast, from where we were anchored, to buy four boys on a Sabbath. The people of the missionary village, near where we anchored, were highly indignant with us for trading, and on the Sabbath. In the evening of the day, we were rowing in a boat for the shore, towards the Christian village, when we were met by a party who fired at us, wounding me in the leg. And we were obliged to return to the ship to bind the boys we had got, to prevent them jumping overboard; and we had to sail away to prevent an attempt at rescue. Now," he said, "what was that for missionary teaching?" I think my readers, unbiassed, will say, "Serve the traders right." They had by foul means—buying from a chief—got possession of four of the islanders. They had openly made light of, and trangressed the keeping, of the Sabbath. And now they were adding insult to injury by making for the Christian village to get hold of more labour men. Trading and seeking to decoy or kidnap on the Sabbath evening. Was it any wonder that these poor fellows, believing to defend their sons and neighbours, and angry because of the transgressing of the Sabbath, should have recourse to arms. But such is not Christian teaching. Nevertheless, many would urge that, as a nation or a village, they would be justified, even on the Sabbath, in repelling the manstealers. Probably other tactics might have been adopted successfully; but what will not a man do when excited, on the spur of the moment, to defend himself, and those near and dear to him, from danger. Atall events, the white men were the aggressors, and under England's flag.

This young man stated that on all voyages, as a rule, one or more lives were lost by firearms. He said : " I went through the love of adventure, and I have been engaged in it for some years ; and it is, to all intents and purposes, truly THE SLAVE TRADE. In it, he had been wounded three times—once in the foot and twice in the leg.

Another labour man on his death bed regretted his evil deeds, and only desired " to live to publicly expose the villainous slave trade."

In the official report of the Fiji Government for the last year—occur some passages thus—

Shots were fired over the head of two recruits who were attempting to escape from the boats of the Lord of the Isles, and a female native who was in the bush was alleged to have been killed.' "' Curio," the boat steerer, and two Fijians from the Taviuni were killed at Santo, and on enquiry before a Deputy of the High Commissioner, the strong presumption appeared, that the incentive arose out of Curios tampering with native women !' ' A second case of the foolish use of firearms took place on board another vessel. In this instance, though several native women were greatly frightened by it, it was satisfactorily established that it was improbable ( ! ! ) that any more serious result had been occasioned.'

Now these three reports put the thing very mildly. The use of firearms simply to frighten a few native women! Perhaps one woman killed ! Simply Curio's tampering with the native women !

At all events, it does allow that with all the legislation, with all the supervision, lives were lost by violence. Murder was committed. The poor captives did try to escape. And no doubt this is and has been oftener the case than otherwise.

And to render the thing much more terrible and dangerous, a bounty has been given in the shape of a musket —and the wages of the men have been paid by a musket, an axe, and a few minor trifles—and so a number of firearms have been gradually introduced into the recruiting grounds, until the natives have felt strong enough to attack inland tribes, and even to fight the man stealer and pirate.

But doubtless many die from violence after capture, and the matter is hood winked. One sailor without shame acknowledged to killing a labour boy off New Caledonia. Two of these boys were talking and insolent. The one told his mate not to do what he was told, as the white man would not dare to touch him. Hearing this and understanding, the sailor ordered him to fill up the cracks between the boards with tar and oakum. He feigned to attempt. The sailor showed him how he wanted the work done and again ordered him to do it. He blankly refused. With that, the sailor daubed the tar brush across his face. She black immediately flew at him, seized a piece of wood and struck at him. He warded off the blow, but received a second on the thigh which knocked him down. Recovering himself, he wrested the piece of wood off the black, and belaboured him with it, and in doing so, knocked him backwards on to the side of the vessel. The fall

broke his back.   Perceiving the state of affairs, the white
man shot his antagonist dead.   The matter was reported
to New Caledonia, but a plea of self-defence was argued,
and a high official said, you did the proper thing, if you
had not succeeded, he would have had your blood.

The above speaks for itself.   If it had been a *bona fide*
master and man engagement, the servant would not have
been insolent, and the master would not have been insult-
ing.   As it was, it was simply one example, of evils insepa-
rable from the veritable slave trade.   But, in this instance,
they were pushed to extremes.

As to the labour vessels :   Only a short time ago, one
was stopped by the Government as unseaworthy ;   and
another I saw myself specially prepared for the trade, was
simply a fraud and a swindle.   But another evil presents
itself in this slave trade which did not in the olden time.
As one of the notes of the Fiji Government report states :
" Two cases of time-expired labourers being landed at the
wrong spot were reported during the season."   Then it
adds :   " How difficult it is, from the ignorance of the
expirees, to guard against this mistake."   Of course it is ;
and the wonder is that so many ever do get back.   Now,
is it possible for men who perhaps have never been to sea
before, or, at all events, rarely far from their own village
to tell after three or more years the exact spot of coast
where their native village is situated.   But the Government report does not, we think, give the outcome of this
mistake—the probability of being killed or eaten ; or, if
this fate be escaped, the chances of a perpetual slavery for
life.   Now, who in their sober senses can call this traffic

a righteous commercial dealing. Thousands are obtained, transported, and subjected to bondage. A large number die in the getting; a large number die during the voyage; a very large proportion die on the plantations; many die by violence when again transhipped to their own group of islands; and few, comparatively speaking, return home safe and sound to their race and kindred.

Morever, by the traffic, diseases are intercommunicated, and thus the physical prowess of the race is lowered and degenerated. A Fijian chief remarked a short time ago: "The English are killing us. We are all dying off, and will soon be gone. They bring diseases, measles, hooping cough, and contagious diseases: and they introduce Polynesians, who bring in and give us other (notably skin) diseases; and we are all dying." And when it is remembered the thousands who died from measles, and the hundreds cut off this very year by hooping cough, and the damage to many by contagious and skin diseases introduced, is it any wonder that he so cried?

The numbers who die, and are thus prevented returning home, naturally opens the eyes of the various islanders. It too often causes suspicion of foul play; so that now it takes a long time for a labour vessel to recruit. The boys are not so easily caught with chaff: and the large introduction of firearms leads them to be more independent; while the wrongs inflicted, directly or indirectly, by the whites lead to retaliation. So that, during the last few years, we have continually been horrified by the news of terrible massacres of white men.

But further: This slave trade, as that of old, by

the muskets given and earned, and, at times, by actual assistance from the whites, enables certain tribes or ambitious chiefs to fight against and lay desolate large numbers of peaceable villages. And such devastation is followed by wholesale murder and cannibalism.

The following, which appears in the July papers of this year, proves the above assertion :—

" By the arrival of the schooner *George Noble* from the Gilbert Group, news has been received of a brutal outrage which has been committed on the natives of Nai Monte Island, by a chief named Abamama and his followers. A number of the Nai Monte islanders are said to have been killed in the conflict, and the stores of English traders seized. The crew of a British schooner, belonging to Auckland, have assisted the chief of the Abamama in the affair."

And it is chiefly to prevent such outrages that philanthropic Britain ought to throw a protectorate over the South Sea Islanders.

Again, in the papers of August 6th, 1884, we have another terrible revelation :

" The mission schooner Ellengowan arrived at Port Moresby to-day, bringing news from New Guinea to 17th July. On the 9th July, the schooner met with H.M.S. gunboat Swinger, at anchor at an island off East Cape. The Queensland labour vessel, Forest King, was there, and had been inspected by the Swinger's officers, and her papers passed, no interpreter being obtainable. On the mission boat coming alongside with an interpreter, it was found that out of fifty men and boys on board, sixteen had escaped in the night by swimming. The magistrate reported this to the commander of the gunboat, who sent the second lieutenant with a crew to take the vessel a prisoner to Cooktown. It is reported that thirty-eight natives have been shot by the crews of the labour vessels on the main land. Besides the *Forest King*, the *Clara*, *Hopeful*, and *Lizzie* had been there. A village had been burnt, and a canoe capsized, and the occupants captured. From one vessel twenty-four natives had attempted to swim ashore, three of whom were drowned. In all cases, even where the natives have voluntarily shipped, the engagement was understood to be for three moons only. The *Swinger* towed the *Ellengowan* for three days round Milne Bay and the Engineer Group, and then proceeded alone to Metape, New Britain, to join the H.M.S. *Diamond*. The natives, so far, had proved friendly, but were suspicious."

A Queensland labour vessel, and not Fijian. But all one system; only up to the present time under a more lenient supervision in Queensland than in Fiji; and so less vigilance exercised to give matters a legal, respectable appearance. And the papers passed by a man-of-war! And how often are the ship's papers passed, and villany legalised, by the Government agents; bribery accomplishing what impudence cannot. But even the irregularities which the Fijian Government do stop, all prove the same nefarious dealing. And how can we expect otherwise than nefarious dealings in a nefarious traffic? What irregularities, almost in a sentence! Village burned; people capsized out of a canoe, and captured; the labour boys swimming ashore when the relieving man-of-war and interpreter came to the rescue. Why then, and not before? What had been the kind and amount of force used to detain them? For it must be apparent to the most casual observer that these poor fellows embraced the first opportunity that offered for regaining their liberty. But more casualties—natives *drowned*; natives *shot*; natives *deceived*; and, on other islands, the natives hitherto friendly, but now becoming suspicious. And was it any wonder? This labour vessel, without any interpreter, and so without the means or power to barter, had got together a number of ignorant, wild savages. How could she do this, excepting by kidnapping and entrapping?

A letter from the first mate of a labour vessel, and for five years in the labour trade, says: "There has never yet been a true book written on 'the slave trade.' I say I have been in the trade a long time, and know that what they call the 'labour trade' is nothing but the old '*slave trade*,' as they bribe them into the boat under false pretences. Often they jump into the water to try and swim ashore, for which they are caught and put in irons. Auckland, New Zealand.—(Signed) THOMAS C. KERRY."

Shortly after the above occurrences, we read again: "The labour schooner Ethel was ordered back from the South Seas by the Government agent on the ground of illegally recruiting, firing on the natives, ill-using the passengers, &c." In fact she had been out for some months on this diabolical mission before she was thus ordered back.

Such like recitals might be multiplied. They speak for

themselves. Philosophically and righteously, only one judgment can be deduced. England's flag has been stained, torn down, and trampled upon, by these impudent slave traffickers of the South Seas.

## FUTURE POLICY, OR THE REMEDIES.

It is easy, comparatively, to mark out national faults and failings, but it is a difficult matter to suggest and create reforms. Where various and varied interests have to be taken into consideration, and where these interests appear more or less to clash, then it needs collective wisdom and experience to steer the State barque safely over all the shoals and quicksands which threaten to destroy.

We have in the South Pacific a number of beautiful islands, peopled by races who, in intelligence and knowledge, are on a parallel with the English public schoolboy. These races, by nature, have sunk to the lowest animalism, degradation, and vice. Since humanity, as a whole, is a common humanity, it behoves philanthropic and civilized nations, if possible, to seek to raise and reform these peoples. It is only possible to reform such fallen people, or, in fact, any morally and socially sunken people, by the means of two powers—fear or love. The former may change the surface, but only the latter can touch the heart. The gospel of civilization is helpless to succeed by means of the forces of love. Selfishness is specially the characteristic of the civilization of the nineteenth century. Commercial competition is too keen to be the pioneer of love, and the pioneers under the flag of civilization are, for the most part, commercial adventurers. They have no powers or forces by which to apply the influences of love. It is against selfish interests to crucify nature and self, by the disinterested propoundings and exhibitions of love. Self suggests to profit upon the ignorance of the savage, by keeping him in the dark as to even a knowledge of the fair value of goods, judged according to the circumstances of the case, and the relations of the parties interested. Men, as civilized commercials, are not very likely to invest their thousands, for the elevation and advancement of the heathen South Sea islanders. From a civilized and worldly view it would not pay, and, in the wisdom of this world, a man so to invest his thousands would be a fanatic and a fool.

It would be but idle words, to urge the savage to imitate commercial civilized ways, and to give up cannibal and other evil practices. He would not see the wisdom of the argument. He would not see the advantages to be gained. He would see no good motive, but only fear and selfishness in the civilized man thus addressing him.

Moreover, a great proportion of the pioneers of civilization, being adventurers, have little character or position to lose. Excepting in murder and cannibalism, they are too often greater blacklegs than the barbarians themselves, and hence any oratory or recommendations from such to reform, would be simply lost on the hearers.

Civilization may conquer barbarians by fear ; but it is powerless to impose rule and dominion over such savages excepting by force. It is powerless to pioneer.

This is well illustrated on the squatting stations in

Queensland. One gentleman, who had bought a station, was continuously being annoyed by raids made by the Australian aboriginals on his cattle. At last matters came to this issue : he must either lose all or else kill the blacks. Conscience would not allow him to do the latter, and so he had to sell his station at a loss.

Another gentleman sought to show his good intentions, by giving parties of blacks a couple of bullocks whenever they visited his station. One day a larger party came, to feast and make merry. He gave them four or five bullocks. After the feast they became extremely excited, and appeared as if possessed with demons. They rushed forth and wantonly speared 150 head of cattle ; and for no purpose, as they simply left them dead where struck down. The issue of civilization, under such circumstances, is that the whites too often become so exasperated, that they kill off these savages whenever they can ; and, consequently, the Australian blacks are fast disappearing.

In fact, the only successful method that could be adopted by pioneers, simply as civilized, would be the rifle and the sword.

It is a well-known fact that the rifle and the sword may strike terror for the time, and in the immediate district ; but they will not prevent revenge, and revenge in the nature of the savage is the strongest passion, and means blood for blood ; and revenge, without power and courage, means cunning and snake-in-the-grass scheming and treachery. Hence, the only way for civilization completely to subdue uncivilized thousands, is to spread terror everywhere by fire and sword, and to tyrannically hold the residue in bondage and slavery.

On the other hand, it has been proved again and again that the Gospel of Christianity can and does transform the savages. There are present no selfish commercial interests to thwart the magic power of the forces of love. The great secret of love's success is self-sacrifice, and in heralding the Gospel of Christianity men and women have to sacrifice self, while they proclaim and lead the intelligences to a higher and heavenly Sacrifice. And thus fortified, they go invincible as a host, until the heathen yield to the power of the *lotu*, and give up their vile customs and their debasing national sins.

And this is not mere assertion. In Fiji the power of love, as manifested under the banner of the Christian cross, has ridded the islands of murder and cannibalism, and transformed the lowest villains into a peaceable, God-fearing people. Rotumah, Samoa, Tonga, all prove the wonderful power of this invincible, irresistible, heaven-born agency ; and, wherever, in the Pacific, Christian missions have been established in philosophic, self-sacrificing philanthropy, the same results have invariably followed.

But note the contrary in New Zealand. There, as in other groups of islands, Missionaries of the Gospel of Peace were the first permanent visitors and settlers. Success attended their efforts. Hundreds of the natives were beginning to *lotu*, and as a proof of their sincerity may be narrated an incident as experienced by the Rev. S. Ironside, one of the pioneer missionaries to New Zealand. At a certain village, where he was the pioneer, and the first white man to penetrate inland, the people in large numbers joined the Church. More than three hundred were admitted in a single year, and that after several months on trial as catechumens. The British and Foreign Bible Society sent out the first issue of New Testaments, printed in the Maori language. Mr. Ironside distributed them among the natives.

One morning, some short time after, he was awakened early by a native urging his presence. Having dressed, he went to see why he was wanted. The man took him outside, and pointed to the hills. There he beheld a stream of people making towards the settlement. Again the native bade him look towards the sea, and, from a distant part of the coast, he beheld a number of canoes also making for the settlement. His astonishment and curiosity were aroused, but the native simply bade him to wait in patience. After a time the different parties arrived, laden with foods, pigs, potatoes, and other articles of commerce. They proceeded to the Mission premises, and there deposited their loads. Then, getting their missionary, Mr. Ironside, to come and inspect them, they told him that they wished to pay the good and thoughtful men in England, who had sent out to them the Word of Life, and so they had brought the goods, that he might sell them and send the money to London. The goods were sold, and realized £35, a sum more than sufficient to pay for all the 500 Testaments. And this was the spontaneous offering of newly-reformed cannibal barbarians. Love begat love. Love created gratitude. Love vitalized the intelligence.

Love kindled in the hearts of these rescued savages a fire which burst into hallowed flame, reaching unto heaven. And to produce such a glorious result, civilization would strive for ever and in vain.

Too early, civilization did come to New Zealand—too early because before the people (excepting in a small minority, and in favoured localities) were Christianized. And what was the issue? Selfish interests warred, and eventually civilization had recourse to power of arms. And in the two New Zealand wars the civilized man, as the stronger, crushed the weaker, and from that period to the present, difficulties have been continuously arising between the two peoples. And the Maoris were not conquered by love, but simply kept in subjection by fear. Civilization here had the most favourable opportunities to transform the Maoris into a peaceable, civilized people. And how miserable the failure! And how more apparent the failure, after the previous successes of Christianizing effort!

And in the islands of the Pacific, civilization is powerless to reform the cannibal, the murderer, the thief, and the vicious; and if civilization have to accomplish the work of transforming, it can only succeed by the aid of physical force, and by a transformation from the barbarian and free to that of the bond and slave. And such will not tend to elevate. Civilization may by such means gain the power to instruct and give knowledge, but knowledge with oppression and discontent is dangerous. And civilization without the Gospel of Christianity means a wider latitude for selfishness and villany, than would

even be decent at home, and a substituting the civilization polite vices, for the ruder and coarser barbarian evils.
Witness French civilization in New Caledonia, where
are evils unfit to mention, and where the national
flag is disgraced by encouraging the natives to capture
and destroy Frenchmen—escaped convicts ! Since then,
it is to the interests of a common humanity that murder,
cannibalism, and internecine wars should cease. It
behoves England to see if it be in her power to
prevent or mitigate such evils. Civilization alone
is too feeble to reform these fallen races,
therefore, before civilization be allowed to lay hold on
these islands, the Gospel of Christianity should be
heralded from shore to shore, and from island to island,
and this as a matter of expediency as well as of righteousness. Whether England believe in Christianity or not,
facts are facts, and wise men and able politicians will
accept facts as such, and frame their actions accordingly.
And since Christianity can and does tame the wild
savage, and thus renders him harmless and humane,
while civilization is powerless to reform or to better his
condition, therefore it is wisdom and philosophy to apply
the restorative for this human woe. But it may be
answered : how does the matter affect England, and what
right has she to interfere? It does affect her, and that in
many ways. As the leading Christian nation, it is her
duty to use her best endeavours to raise fallen humanity,
and to prevent war and massacre. As the home of
freedom and philanthropy, it behoves her to spread her
wings of protection and goodwill over the weak and

oppressed. As a commercial nation, it behoves her to rid the South Seas of pirates and man-stealers, rogues, and vagabonds. As a nation of colonies, it behoves her, in the true interests of her Australian possessions, and through them her own interests, to throw a protectorate over all the islands of the South Pacific. This is necessary to the preventing other nations officiously interfering, and introducing all the evils of a mere civilization. It is also necessary to prevent the unjust, rapacious dealings of many so-called traders, and the unrighteous acts of the labour traffickers. Look at the effects of a mere civilization. Look at the sensual vices of Noumea, the Sodom of the South Pacific. Is it any wonder that within the last fifty years the native inhabitants of New Caledonia have decreased fifty per cent? And wherefore this French colonization—not for the national honour, not for the national advancement of France, but as a cesspool wherein to throw all her abominations and villany, and that close to the doors of England's largest colonies—Australian, Tasmanian, and New Zealand colonies. And as contiguity to a seething cesspool means an exposure to deadly disease germs, so the contiguity of the Australian colonies, to this abode of vices and crime, must mean the inoculating the healthy atmosphere of these southern climes with noxious germs. And hence we see English adventurers growing rich by popularizing vice, and seducing simple-minded unsuspicious girls, from the colonies, to the lusts and villanies of these Frenchmen; while the criminal classes of the colonies are augmented and vilified by the addition of numbers of escaped convicts and *libérés*. If, then, one civilized spot already cause so much evil by its foulness, what would be the effect of a multiplication of similar evils, and under the ordering of different nations, and this evil augmented by the intricate workings of the slave trade? Further, the English being the true colonizers, have the trade with New Caledonia mostly in their hands. The mining and other enterprizing companies are English or Colonial. This gives rise to great jealousy and bad feeling on the part of the French. Only a few weeks ago, the Governor who has just left, tore down from the wall of a native hut, the portrait of the Queen of England, as presented in the " Graphic" newspaper. And this he did, with words and acts unfit to mention in connection with such dealing.

The wrongs committed by the slave hunters and too often unscrupulous traders, upon the various islanders have, in too many instances, led these people to seek redress by vengeance upon the innocent. Whites committed the wrong, whites must be punished —blood for blood ; and thus often such retribution has led to further complications. A man-of-war, looking at the matter one-sidedly, has punished the peoples for exercising, as they believed, righteous revenge ; and this is going on until now it is uncertain whether the natives, on many a coast in the different groups, will be friendly or hostile to any visiting whites. Thus matters are continuously becoming more complicated, the savages are being rendered more savage, commercial dealings more hazardous, the reforming these islanders a more difficult matter, and the safety of life and property more uncertain in these Seas ; and in the future, unless the evils be crushed in the bud, and especially if other nations come in, serious complications must arise affecting the Australian colonies, and, through them, indirectly or otherwise—even directly—England herself. America had to learn the lesson of humanity through a baptism of blood ; England, through her West Indian colonies, had to pay the price for the same by a score of millions of pounds. Will she need another lesson, or will she now in wisdom crush the evils in the bud, stop the slave trade altogether, throw a protectorate over the South Sea islands, and in boldness and righteousness declare to all nations, for once and all, the fundamental basis of a peace-preserving and unselfish foreign policy ? Annexation, without previously taming the wild men, would incur endless difficulties. In fact, as shown, it is impossible to tame and elevate the islanders, by a mere civilization annexation ; but let missions be established under a British protection ; let the heathen lands be flooded with native teachers from Fiji, Tonga, and other Christianized groups. And such men and true can be found, and willing to face death and danger, in seeking to take the Gospel of Christianity to heathens and cannibals.

And these men can be fitted out and sent for the small sum of £20 each per annum.

To show the true heroism resulting, even in native character, from the revealed and taught philosophy of the Gospel of Christianity, I may relate the following :—

In one of the heathen islands, a chief wishing to

embrace Christianity sent for a teacher. The greater part of the people were opposed to the change, and declared the teacher, when sent, should not land alive. In Lakemba the superintendent minister laid the state of affairs before the quarterly (one of the Church's) meetings. He depicted the terrors of the heathenism and its surroundings, and then asked specially for a volunteer to carry the Gospel to the village where the would-be murderers lived. A man named Moses got up and, with his eyes full of tears, cried, " send me." He was urged to reconsider his decision. It was pointed out to him that the going almost meant certain death —that he would need to bid farewell to his country and his friends. But remonstrance was useless, and, with the tears now streaming down his face, as he spoke of the love of his Saviour to himself, and his desire to give his life, even to the death, in sacrifice to Him, he declared that he must and would go. He went. As the ship neared the shore and cast anchor a boat was lowered. But the boat had to be kept back. The shore was lined with natives in hostile attitude, and, from their gestures and screams, together with the goodly array of spears and clubs, and bows and arrows, there could be no mistaking their feelings and intentions. Word was given to sail away, and express command not to allow Moses to go on shore. Moses pleaded in vain : the captain would not risk his life nor the lives of the crew. But Moses was not to be done, and so, holding up a New Testament in one hand for the natives to see, and having wrapped his garment about his waist, he sprang thus defended, and yet defenceless, into the sea and swam for the shore. The natives were awed—an unseen influence rendered them helpless—a mighty power preserved Moses from harm. And thus, armed and yet unarmed, mighty yet weak, feeble in culture and education, yet strong in faith and valorous by grace, he overcame a multitude, and by the forces of love conquered the terrors of evil. Moses conquered. What heroism! What valour! What a halo of glory appears to descend upon his noble brow, as we see him struggling with the waves and swimming for the shore!

Yes, Christianity, even through the instrumentality of an unrefined, uncultured Fijian, can work wonders; and wonders, such as civilization could never effect, a complete and a bloodless victory.

In the beautiful island of Viwa, the most horrible cannibalism prevailed. The Rev. John Hunt and others wrought and lived continuously for the moral elevation of this people. But they seemed hardened as hard as stone. Revolting scenes were continuously enacted before his very door, and the lives of himself and wife were often in jeopardy and danger. But the heathen, although so depraved and fallen, were keen judges of character. They could not but perceive the self-denying character of the mission families' lives and works. And at last a mighty power came over them. The strong men fainted when they beheld in the light of heaven the heinousness of their sins. For a time they were prostrate, overwhelmed in physical weakness. Whole towns were laid low in sorrow and anguish. But at last there came a mighty peace—a calm trust on the full efficacy of the sacrificial atonement. And from that time heathenism ceased. What a wondrous power, this manifestation of love, as preached to the cannibals in the lives of the mission families, and as manifested to them direct from heaven! It rooted out the degrading vices of heathenism. It tamed the wild men of Viwa. And in all history the same experiences are repeated. Christianity can subdue by the powers of love; but civilization can only hold in check by fear, and crush by force of arms and bloodshed.

If England then act wisely, philosophically, and philanthropically, she will send missionary agencies to all the islands in the Pacific, and in such numbers as soon to thoroughly Christianize and evangelize all the populations.

Then, and only then, excepting by recourse to arms, and in continued danger of loss of life, will communication and intercourse with these peoples be safe.

Let Christianity first tame the savage, and then civilization under, a righteous government, may safely follow in its train.

But further, civilization, as understood by Europeans, or the training the South Sea island natives into European ways, is dangerous, even if preceded by the teachings of Christianity. These natives have only capacity equal to the public schoolboy, and to lift them up to the ways of English refinement, is to deteriorate from their moral worth. A native squats on the matting on the floor, but put him on a chair and he at once manifests the faults of a spoilt child. He becomes too big for himself or for anyone else.

Put him in European clothes and he is simply beside himself. Give him a knife and fork to eat with, and he becomes superior to you, and allows impudence and foppishness to drive away good manners and self-respect. His boylike capacities cannot bear the too sudden exaltation or excited strain. His brain becomes turned with foolish pride and the man becomes offensive, impudent, and useless. And even as too much learning may make the physically weak European mad, so too much civilization makes the Polynesian morally and socially mad. Such a one completely loses his head, and becomes a fool. He cannot bear the (to him) too sudden elevation.

To succeed, then, the truest philosophic and philanthropic policy is first to tame the wild man by means of the forces innate to the Christian Gospel, next to give him the simplicities only, or the alphabet of civilization, raise him from the stone age to the iron age, give him knives, hatchets, spades, and other simple implements for agriculture or the minor arts. Teach him reading and writing in his own language, as well as the elements of arithmetic, history, and geography. On no account teach him English. The knowledge makes him too uppish and disagreeable. Discourage European clothing, excepting a light shirt for the men, for the Sabbath and festivals, and a light bodice for the women on like occasions. And it is astonising how becoming the natives look, simply wearing the sulu round the middle on ordinary occasions and working days, and with a light shirt or bodice on extra occasions—worship or festival. In a word, without interfering with harmless native customs, elevate them spiritually, but put them in a position so as to raise themselves in civilization by natural efforts from within—efforts growing from necessity, or as the outcome of increasing knowledge and developing capacities—efforts entirely created within their own native community, and thus natural, gradual, and stable. It should be always remembered that civilization, as matured and refined amongst the English, is a dangerous thing for Fijians or Polynesians, until generations of experience shall have reframed their characters, and developed various mental capacities. But, in the meantime, let England throw a protectorate over the groups of South Sea islands, for various reasons—

1. For staying the so-called labour traffic, or, in its true term, the slave trade.

2. For giving a certain amount of moral protection to the missionary pioneers and agents.

3. For preventing tribal wars and systematic invasions, devastation, and cannibalism.

4. For restricting white settlement, excepting judiciously, and when to the advantage of both peoples.

5. For seeking to establish central governments, with more or less nominal power, sufficient to prevent or punish massacres, murder, and rapine.

6. For seeking to regulate trade and preventing piracy and marauding.

A Pacific commissionate should be over the whole, with ships of war cruising between the various islands, with power to punish offenders and redress grievances.

In the above recommendations I have simply named a

protectorate. Of course, circumstances might arise in which it might be desirable in the interests of peace and mutual advantage, where annexation would be the wiser policy; but such must depend upon the circumstances. Each plan has its advantages. In a protectorate the native government would necessarily be patriarchal, and thus the advance of the people slower, while difficulties might arise from time to time, which would not occur under annexation.

Annexation would demand an increased outlay. It would, however, enable the gradual undermining of the patriarchal system and a raising of the people by encouraging individual efforts, and by establishing and protecting individual rights. It would make the position of the peoples safer from the attack or caprices of foreign nations or evil-disposed whites. But, to secure all the benefits, it would need to be preceded by Christianizing the people generally, and this could be the better brought about under a protectorate. To annex the islands without previously taming the wild man, and to seek to civilize under such conditions, would lead to endless difficulties and troubles, and would necessitate the use of arms and a greater or less loss of life and concomitant evils. A nominal annexation, without allowing white settlement— excepting official—or colonization, would be a step in advance of a protectorate. But to make it successful, it should be worked harmoniously with the Christianizing missions—the savage taming agencies.

Most assuredly, the labour traffic, as it is politely called—but, in truth, the slave trade—should be put a

stop to at once, and England should be true to her
colours and keep to her former proclamation and flag
—to sweep the seas of such traffic, no matter under what
national flag, or however fictitious the colours under
which the traffic exists. The natives have not the
wisdom and understanding, to be in a position, to engage
as hired servants. The Government *cannot*, by laws
or regulations, *wash a black spot white*. They cannot,
with ignorance on the part of the blacks, and with self
interests and unscrupulous cunning on the part of the
traffickers, prevent injustice, man-stealing, man-buying,
rapine, and murder. Therefore, the sooner they put a
stop to the whole system, the better for all parties,
though, in doing so, present interests should be respected;
and, at the expiration of the period of service, the
Polynesians should be free to return home or re-engage
as they pleased. But how is labour to be obtained?
The Government are bringing in a number of Indian
coolies, but, unfortunately, the agents are not careful
to hire respectable men, and hence many bad characters
and most immoral, are turned loose in Fiji. It can,
doubtless, be easily proved that the Chinese are better
workers than the coolies. But there are two drawbacks with John and his followers—his opium
smoking and his open immorality—to say nothing of
his uncleanly domestic habits. But, as Fiji is a Crown
colony, a law could be framed forbidding the use of
opium to the Chinaman. Reliable agents in China
could engage married men, and men not addicted to

opium smoking, and with the knowledge that opium would be a thing forbidden in Fiji.

And, as regards the domestic arrangements, the difficulty occurs also with the coolies, many of whom are terribly slovenly and uncleanly; but the giving them commodious houses, and the general supervision of their domestic arrangements, would quickly and largely mitigate this evil. Too often the coolie is not only slovenly, but lazy, and will feign illness—screaming, doubling up, and by other manœuvres seeking to deceive the doctor and to be put on the sick list; whereas, perhaps, and certainly under tropical skies, there is not a more patient, quiet, industrious worker than the Chinaman.

The question of importing white labour is most difficult. White men are ambitious, and the working man would as a rule, rather starve on nothing than work for four instead of five shillings a day. Then, again, the market question must in future seriously disturb the sugar industry of Fiji. There is now such a sugar craze that the rivalry between companies and interests in Mauritius, Queensland, and other sugar producing countries will lead to a large fall in the price of sugar. The manufacture of beetroot sugar also enters into competition. A broker assured me a few days ago that sugar selling a short time ago at £31 per ton had dropped several pounds per ton, and, as demand and supply act and react upon each other, when the supply is over the demand, prices drop; and the large creation of the industry in Queensland and Fiji, in addition to those previously established in other countries, and which have hitherto satisfied the

demand, must—and especially as it develops—lead to a
surplus supply.   And, as the weakest first go to the wall,
Fiji and Queensland must be the first to suffer.

In the interests of all parties, it behoves the Fijian
Government to regulate the sugar industry, by not allowing large monopolies of land, by encouraging other
industries, and by legislating wisely with a view of right-
ing all classes of peoples.

As matters stand at present, they are most unsatisfac-
tory.   The sugar companies holding mills are a cause of
strife instead of a blessing to the country.   They get
their commodities from the Australian colonies or direct
from England, and so do not, by trading, benefit Fiji.
In fact, they stand in a position that, excepting the
actual cost of the sugar-cane, and a small percentage of
Fiji labour, they bring little or no money into Fiji.
On the  other hand,  they are continuously harvesting
money and sending it abroad, draining the country.
Again, they made an agreement with the small planters for
a supply of cane for ten years, at the price of ten shillings
a ton.   Labour then rose in price, and so the planters
say they cannot sell, without ruin, for the money.   Then,
again, the planters reckoned on raising three crops of
cane in two years, but the sugar companies, on the
advice of experts, leave the cane some months in the fields
to mature, and hence the planters look upon this as
an injustice—the keeping their lands idle so as to secure
a better article and at no higher figure for the seller.
But, further, it is reckoned that at present rates and with
all drawbacks the planters may make £2 (two pounds)

per acre per annum out of their land. But small planters
consider this insufficient to pay them for outlay, cost of
living, and their own supervision. And what must it be
as, after a short time, the land will need deeper ploughing
or manuring? And amid all the exigencies of the case—
the rising of wages, the dearness of provisions, the falling
in prices for sugars, and other difficulties, what guarantee
has the grower for comparative comfort, to say nothing of
the great probabilities of losing all his little capital and
settled home?

I was informed for a positive fact that a high government official, who had been largely instrumental in
securing the establishment of colossal sugar companies,
had acknowledged that, instead of a benefit, they had
brought a bear into the country. Be this as it may, the
fact remains that by them the resources and wealth of the
country is largely drawn upon, and exported to other lands
instead of benefiting the country itself. It is necessary
to profit by received lessons. In the time of the
American war a cotton mania seized upon the people, and
for one year, when they could obtain 4s. a pound, the
growers did very well, and the cotton was doubtless the
finest in the world. But when the war ceased and
cotton could again be run into the English markets at
1s. 4d. (sixteenpence) a pound, then the Fijian growers
were ruined.

Little attention has been as yet given to agriculture,
but there is a quantity of beautiful grass all the year
round in Fiji, and cattle appear to thrive well. Pigs,
also, as is well known, flourish in Fiji, and yet the whites

import bacon and salt pork, paying twopence per pound duty. Taro (ndalo) and yams, similar to our potato, can be cultivated, and at a high remuneration; yet the whites almost entirely trust to the natives for the supply, or else import potatoes. Cocoanuts might be grown to a much greater extent than at present, as nuts or copra would always find a good market. Bananas and pine apples could be grown in any number, and a trade secured with the colonies by employing small, fast steamers, specially built for carrying such fruits, and with the least destructive loss. Poultry might be bred in large numbers, and so supply to a great extent the necessary change required, from the continuous use of imported tinned meats. Fish swarm in the rivers and seas, but are neglected as an article of diet. Maize might be grown in much larger quantity than at present. In fact, the white people generally do not pay the careful and scientific attention to diet which they ought to do. They live too artificially considering the climate; they seek to follow the luxurious diet of the Australian colonies—meat three times a day—and that meat too often tough, fresh-killed beef, or haggard, shrunken, sea-sick, half-starved mutton. When this is not available all sorts of tinned beefs, mutton, kidneys, salmon, &c., have to do service. Vegetable production is neglected, and the scarcity or absence of such is a serious item. Fruits—such a natural diet in Fiji—are too often plucked before ripe, and thus give rise to dysentery, a sort of low fever, and other ailments. While staying at an hotel shortly after my arrival I indulged in a large Fiji orange. It was quite sour.

I afterwards went to the shore for a walk, and examination
of sea-side treasures.　Gradually I felt myself losing
power and strength.　The sun was more oppressive to me,
than at any other time while in the islands.　I was in
a burning heat, and, although I had only proceeded about
half a mile, it was with the greatest difficulty that I got
back to quarters.　For two days I was unfit to get about,
or to collect specimens, and, no doubt, all owing to my
eating an unripe orange—the proper way, we are told, to
eat fruit in Fiji !　Some time afterwards, in the garden
of a native village, I was able to feast upon any number
of luscious, ripe oranges, and with no ill effects.　The
matter of diet is noticeable more especially among the
children.　They grow up winey, puny, pale-faced—thin,
weak, and fragile—and not so much because of the
climate as because of the diet.　I observed one such
youthful hope.　His daily routine was—

Breakfast—Fries or stews, vegetables, preserved fish,
jam and bread (not bread and jam), and a finish up
with bananas and oranges.

Lunch—Soup, stewed rabbit, cold meats, sweets, jam
and bread, bananas, and oranges.

Dinner—Soup, hot joints, prepared meats, tarts, jam
and bread, tea, bananas, and oranges.

And, between meals, a walk of perhaps two hundred
yards, a loll, and a nap.

But, of course, for persons arrived at maturity, must be
added their beers and grog, and we must not forget the
billiards and card-playing, and accompanying late hours.

On the other hand, look at the natives.　They live

chiefly on a vegetable diet, undisturbed in digestive activity by beers and grog. At times they vary this diet with pork, poultry, and fish. They go to rest early, and rise with the dawn of day; and, probably, a finer race of men physically cannot be found on the face of the earth. They are roundly developed, without obesity. Their muscles stand out in bold relief. Their digestion is excellent, and they are jocular, jolly, and void of dull cares. No liver complaints appear to cause nervousness or harassing anxiety. They eat well, they sleep well, and they look the pictures of happiness.

It is astonishing how rapidly severe wounds heal. Nearly all the natives exhibit long scars, chiefly on the muscles of the back and shoulders, less often on the legs and arms. These were self-inflicted, or inflicted by the person's consent. They were bantered or dared into thus hacking themselves—bantered to prove themselves game to bear the suffering, and like children, without moral courage, afraid of being laughed at. They are acute enough to select the fleshy parts of the body. But it is a wonder how they avoid cutting or wounding the various arteries. They not only cut open, deep, and long gashes, but also keep open the same by irritants. Thus the wound heals slowly, granulating from the base and forming broad, conspicuous scars, which, ever after, proclaim to all, their pluck and power of endurance. Certain it is that the punishment which they thus undergo would kill many English people—yet these islanders are not even laid up.

I was highly amused at the result of medical advice in a disabled English islander. The medical adviser stated that his patient wanted more vegetable diet, and ordered him, whenever he got the chance, to indulge freely in salads and green stuff ; a glass of spirits to aid digestion. I had the pleasure or pain of dining with this said gentleman, and was somewhat amused to see the onslaught which he made on the lettuce, onions, sliced beetroot, etc. In the course of the afternoon I found him helplessly helpless, in a half-comatose state, unlike drunkenness, and unlike the symptoms of a fit. I learned that he had followed the doctor's instructions to the letter, and really sought to cure his sluggish liver by the salad and grog prescription. As he was on the verge of a fit, and as I expected a case, I certainly thought that at last doctors were copying lawyers, in making work for each other.

No doubt Fiji is an enervating climate, and the European should have periodic change, either in a good sea voyage, or by a visit to the colonies or to England. But, as a whole, the evils of the climate have been greatly exaggerated, and many of the ailments consequent on diet and drink are blamed on the climate. Oftentimes the air is damp and much rain falls, but the temperature generally ranges from 78 deg. to 84 deg., rarely sinking to 68 deg. or rising to 90 deg. ; and in the day the sun dispels the dampness, and at night breezes from the sea cool the air. Such a climate should not tell seriously upon Europeans, with ordinary care, and attention to diet and clothing. Meat once a day, and varied by poultry, fish, and game, would be sufficient to give

tone and energy, while a liberal, varied vegetable and
ripe fruit diet should give muscle and strength.    Absti-
nence from intoxicating liquors is specially needful in
the tropics, as, where life lives so fast, man has no
strength to waste in exchange for the pleasurable sensa-
tions produced by alcoholic stimulants.   Not as an old
Scotchman put it to me.   He witnessed my buying a
flask of whisky.   "Yes," he said, "you will require
some of the needful to stay the inner man when on
your hunting expeditions.   As it was, I found my specimens of spiders, bugs, beetles, etc., needed it more than
myself, and so I unselfishly divided it among them.
Taken as a whole, Fiji is a beautiful place for a wealthy
Australian to winter.   It has numerous drawbacks,
social and political, and it is certainly not the place for
a man with a little capital to go to, if he expects to sit at
ease, waited upon by black labour, and to make a rapid
fortune.   But, with all its disadvantages, a family with a
little capital, and capable of honest work and thrift, can
doubtless make a comfortable living in a small way.   A
limited number of storekeepers and little traders can here
find scope ;   and small farmers, in keeping banana,
cocoanut, and orange plantations, or in growing pine-
apples and other fruits and vegetables, should make a fair
business.   But while labour is so uncertain, and while
government is so feeble, the fewer the better, the white
people who risk to lose a fortune in Fiji.

Many of the Government laws need reforming.   A
very beneficial law, and a wise one, is that the natives

shall not be supplied with or treated to alcoholic stimulants, excepting under a penalty of fifty pounds (£50). But the feeble policy, either of fear or of fawning to the chiefs, comes in, and a clause provides that a permit may be given by the Government to a chief. Of course, if they·are afraid or jealous of the chiefs, they could not adopt a better plan to get rid of them ; but such policy is feeble, and ill-becoming the representatives of her Majesty the Queen. An amusing and yet sad illustration of the jumbling together of evil and good regulations occurred just previously to my visit. A man who was friendly with a chief, and had received favours from him, gave this chief, when visiting him, some drink. The report got abroad ; the man was brought up and fined the fifty pounds. Now, it is stated that the chief told his host that he had a permit, and so the host, perhaps by this thrown off his guard, had to suffer through the permits being one part of the law. Another most foolish clause permits natives to fetch alcoholic liquors if they carry a written order. But a person was fined the fifty pounds a short time ago for selling to a native, because—so report guarantees—there was no date upon the written order. Now the wisdom which does not know, that the allowing children to play with matches, has often led to a fire and the burning down a house, is not the wisdom needed to give laws to Fiji, under the name of the British Crown. And are not Government, in forbidding Europeans to give natives drink, and yet allowing natives to go for the same and to carry it away, but playing a childish game? Is it really a fact, that the Europeans are become so enervated, that they cannot order their own liquors or go for the little at a time themselves? Let the sale or gift of alcoholic drinks to the natives be punishable with the severe penalty of £50, but let the chiefs also enjoy the blessing, and do not let the law be a dead letter, by giving the carriers of drinks the opportunity to take a little drop, even under the onus of stealing what does not belong to them.

The open licentiousness of the whites, and especially of many of the Government officials, should be stopped by law. As it is, owing to the small salaries given, the imagined drawbacks of the climate, the distance from home, and for other reasons, Fiji has to be satisfied with an all-round inferior class of Government officials. Many are seekers of employment, who failed in the Civil Service examinations in the old country, and who, in answer to friendly influence and numerous solicitations, are dotted down on to this out of the way colony. Of course there are some few exceptions, and where the Government servant lives and behaves as a gentleman; but the general conduct is pompous, affected, uncivil, and domineering, as far as they dare, to the whites, and especially so to the natives. Many of them are better adepts at their beers, and at billiards and cards, and at late hours, filthy conversation, and swearing, than they are at their business. But, be this as it may, Government cannot interfere with a man's private life, excepting by removing or degrading him, if his habits prevent his attention to business. But, in Fiji, where the British Government have agreed to act, as guardian and protectorate to the natives, drunkenness should be most severely punished, and the open licentiousness, in keeping concubines of the Poly‑nesian women, should be stopped. In a free land the government are not justified in interfering with a man's private and domestic life; but in a Crown colony, specially instituted for the safeguard of the natives, it becomes an imperative duty to stop the evil example of open licen‑tiousness. Why should an impudent, selfish fop, if even he may come of a good family, be allowed to set a most debasing example of animal sensualism, before the native races, and openly and boastfully? and why should he be relieved from the honourable relationships of marriage, and allowed to overflow the country with half-caste and illegitimate children? The thing is most monstrous; and, as if to countenance and legitimize such practice, the chiefs are allowed to do the same. At the council lately held one chief, shocked by such liberties being granted, spoke of the matter, and was quietly answered, it was the ancient custom of the country. But wherefore has England come, to enable the chiefs to live at ease, to drink fire water, and to brutalize their women in sensual concubinage? Is it to permit rakeish young good-for-nothings at home, to fly into a Moslem's fools' paradise? Certainly not; such is a disgrace to England's flag, and the sooner the law steps in the better.

The tax of £1 per head to be paid by the natives may be looked upon as an equivalent to a house and land tax. But here again the freedom of the native is interfered with. As a bondman, he is compelled, under the power of the chief, to grow vegetable products, which are to be collected, sent to Government stores, and sold ; the natives to be debited at the small sum of £1 per man, and the remainder, if any, to be handed over to the chiefs. Now, it very often happens, that the produce goes to decay, or depreciates in value before Government sell it. The result is an injustice to the natives, who have to supply another consignment. Again, when an overplus is paid, instead of being distributed equally among the contributing villages, it is largely shared with the chiefs, lieutenant of the town, and other officials, and so the poor natives may really often pay twice or thrice the value of their pound in kind for taxes. Provided £1 (one pound) per head is paid, why should Government interfere with the liberty, communal and individual, and compel each district to keep the public garden, and to waste an amount of time, as the whim or caprice of the public gardener may suggest, in growing produce for taxes ? The Wesleyan missionaries obtain a large free-will offering for the maintenance of foreign missions in coin, and by simply appealing to the good instincts of the people. If righteous, certainly levy a poll-tax of £1, but, so long as it is paid, do not render the burden heavier by red-tape interference ; and, when paid, secure to the natives advantages commensurate with the value received. Let them see it is an impost for their own good, and no doubt it will be willingly forthcoming, and without the interference and injustice as at present.

In a Crown colony, and offering such a number and variety of difficulties as Fiji does, it behoves the English Government to secure, and to send out the best political and statesmanship talent obtainable ; and such talent should receive its rightful remuneration. Moreover, the Civil Service should not be a mere playground into which to send inferior class youths. All offices should be well filled and well paid.

The medical service should be revised. At present the chief medical officer is often not available, inasmuch as he has to steer so many of the offices of State. He receives a name for skill, but of what avail is a name, if the personage be hampered with political offices and duties? The pay given to medical officers—of whom there are ten for all the Fijis—is absurdly small, and so it cannot be expected otherwise, than that youths without experience or practice, would for the most part be the only gentlemen available under such circumstances.

One small piece of terrorism, a disgrace to England and to the profession, came under my notice. A chemist, as chemists sometimes will, placed a stethoscope to the chest of a man, and gave a bottle of medicine. He received a sharp letter, telling him not to repeat such practice, or he would be *deported!* So far, so good. But, not content with this, patients were ordered not to give him their prescriptions to make up, under the pain of having those prescriptions torn up; and a club for which he put up medicines was threatened to be left without medical attendance, unless they transferred their patronage to another chemist. The man was simply persecuted and hounded, until he took to drink in his anger and desperation. Such meanness ill becomes the medical profession. There is great need of a thorough reformation in this line, and registered medical practitioners should have free scope to practice, separate from Government influence in Fiji as a Crown colony.

Sir Arthur Gordon, it appears, started with the belief that it was essential to Fijian life, and to the safety of the English colonists, that the chiefs should be kept in power. Hence they were appointed to offices under the English Government, but politicians, as well as philosophers, know that two governments, and on different lines of policy, cannot run parallel and smoothly together. A man and his wife, even though joined in matrimony, cannot rule their household wisely and successfully if their policies clash, and unless they rule as one. Partners cannot make a business succeed, if their views and acts contradict each other. And so the English Government and the Fijian chiefs cannot rule side by side in full authority. Consequently, too often through fear, or through mistaken policy, the English Government give up their position, and leave matters in the hands of the chiefs, who, it is thus hoped, will consolidate the people to British rule ; and by this policy the patriarchal bondage is upheld, and the people are, in truth, socially and politically slaves. A most absurd issue of the Government tactics was witnessed a few weeks ago. It appears that a native Fijian to be allowed to work for Europeans must exhibit his name on a public roll before his fellow-townsmen. He has then to get the consent of the various chiefs, and lastly of the Government. A number of hands were required for labour. The Government sent a messenger to Kandavu. Knowing his way about, this able young man, by a promise of a pound a head present bounty, soon procured the hands. By dint of management and making it worth their while, he obtained the consent of the chiefs. The boys were shipped and landed at Suva. All appeared ready, but upon the Government inquiry, Were these men registered as seeking for employment? the answer was, no. Then send them all back, as the Government cannot allow such an irregularity. But, though not registered, at the seeking of Government, and with the consent of the chiefs, the boys wished to come, and have come. Send them back at once, was the imperative reply. The men on the beach met the Government recruiter, and stated their repugnance to going back under the circumstances, and asking to be allowed to take any work in Suva: but no, although British subjects they were denied British liberty, and the poor fellows, as sheep, had to be marched back, so to speak, after inspection, to please the whims of a red tape, facetious Government.

Here, then, is an anomaly—British subjects slaves on British soil! What is the remedy? A righteous, bold, and independent policy. Let the Fijian, as the Briton, and himself a British subject, be free. Let the independent power of the chiefs gradually wane. Let the British Government, as supreme, perform their duties, but righteously. Let the offices under Government be elective and periodic, so as to allow the natives to put in their best men. Let the Fijian commoner, as the English husbandman, be at liberty to take work in his own neighbourhood, without the interference or permission of his town or tribal chief ; let him, with proper safeguards, be free to take work at a distance from home in his own or neighbouring islands, provided he takes with him his wife and family. Then the whites, as English employers of labour, cannot ask more, and the family relations will be maintained, and further, the people will be begin to understand and to value the possession of property : and, as to breaking up the present villages, the planters would not be able to obtain the men by bribery, or promises of such, for it would only pay them to seek for honest labour—man with man : and, labour and wages being equalized, value for value, the probability is that at first, very few would go to any distance from their own village, but if at any time they should migrate in any large proportions, and probably only to good masters, then it would simply be the removal of the village site, and to the protection and shelter of the plantation and habitations of the whites. But, while giving the Fijian these privileges, remember his childhood, and guard him personally and socially.

1. By having the compact under Government supervision.

2. By regulating the hours of labour, and thus securing to the man, if near enough to his home, a residence and time with his family.

3. If distant from his native township, to guarantee a native house and parcel of garden ground sufficient for his own requirements, and the maintenance and residence of his wife and family on the estate.

4. To have all the estates under Government supervision, with authority to receive complaints from master or man direct, and power to adjudge and deal with the same.

5. If necessary, to grant a holiday periodically, as Saturday afternoons, or otherwise as required, for the transaction of private business, family, and social.

6. That the compact be to the advantage of both parties, that the wages be paid to the labourer every Saturday, and that the service be free, notice of cessation to be given by either side so many days or weeks beforehand, as agreement according to the nature of the work or the interests of the parties.

7. That the natives be not answerable to the chiefs, either as obtaining their consent, or as in paying to them the whole or any of their wage.

8. That a native may hire himself out at any time for a day, or on piecework, and without the consent of the chiefs.

Thus the native would be free and independent. The chieftain bondage broken in this and other ways would gradually give place to the righteous government of the English, and under the flag of religious, social, and political liberty.

A council should be formed, nominated or elected periodically by the natives themselves, for the framing and keeping in vogue such laws as, under English jurisdiction, would tend to elevate or benefit their people ; and these laws, approved by the English Government, and

compatible with English institutions and charters and
Fijian rights, should be carried out by the Government
in the interests of the natives. Their Sabbath should be
respected; their religious creeds should be upheld and
defended; their religious services and innocent national
customs should be respected; and, as a *finale* and
summing up, righteous laws should be framed and
administered for the joint benefit and protectorship, as
well as for the separate interests, of both white man and
black. Not needless interference and dogmatic domineering, but the caring for the community as a whole,
and for each race as a people, and with the object of
guarding and still further advancing each individual
member of each race socially, morally, and intellectually;
but above all, to secure and *uphold the glories of
England's name in social, political, and religious liberty!*

J. C. MITCHELL, PRINTER, SOUTH MELBOURNE.